D0068317

CATHOLIC WOMEN SPEAK

CATHOLIC
WOMEN
SPEAK

Bringing Our Gifts to the Table

Edited by the
Catholic Women Speak Network

Paulist Press
New York / Mahwah, NJ

Cover image: background texture photo by nopparatz/depositphotos.com
Cover design by Tamian Wood
Book design by Lynn Else

Library of Congress Control Number: 2015948018

ISBN 978-0-8091-4974-2 (paperback)
ISBN 978-1-58768-603-0 (e-book)

Published by Paulist Press
997 Macarthur Boulevard
Mahwah, New Jersey 07430
www.paulistpress.com

Printed and bound in the
United States of America

CONTENTS

Foreword: Of Listening Ears and Prophetic Voices..................xi
    Agbonkhianmeghe Orobator, SJ

Preface..xvii

Contributors..xix

Introduction xxvii
    Editorial Team

Abbreviations xxxiii

Part One—
Traditions and Transformations 1

Introduction to Part One 3

Women in the Church: Models of the Past—
    Challenges of Today..7
    Cettina Militello

The Catholic Intellectual Tradition and
    Women Theologians..11
    Ursula King

Imago Dei: Sexual Difference and Human Becoming 15
    Janet Martin Soskice

Jesus and Women: "You Are Set Free".......................................19
    Elizabeth A. Johnson

Who Is Christ for African Women? 23
    Anne Arabome

Latin American Women: In Mary's Footsteps or
   in Her Shadow? 27
   Carolina del Río Mena

The Motherhood of the Church: Mary,
   the Quotidian, and the People of God................................32
   Cristina Lledo Gomez

Traditions and Transformations: Catholic and
   Muslim Women in Dialogue..37
   Trish Madigan

PART TWO—
Marriage, Families, and Relationships 41

Introduction to Part Two 43

Catholics, Families, and the Synod of Bishops:
   Views from the Pews 51
   Julie Clague

Catholic Families: Theology, Reality, and the Gospel.............57
   Lisa Sowle Cahill

The Love That Crosses Lines: The Graced
   Transgressions of Family Life 62
   Clare Watkins

What on Earth Can Complementarity Actually Be?................67
   Sara Maitland

Saint Anne: A Saint for Today?--A Reflection on
   Grandmothers and Holy Families.......................................70
   Tina Beattie

Welcome but Not Welcome: Going to Mass with
   My Baptist Husband 75
   Margaret Watson

Marriage and Divorce: Telling Our Stories—Marriage and
   Divorce through the Eyes of a Child 77
   Alison Concannon Kennedy

Contents

Marriage and Divorce: Telling Our Stories—
Traumatic Divorce and Sacramental Healing......................80
Pippa Bonner

Marriage and Divorce: Telling Our Stories—
A Very Faithful Rebel...83
Anna Cannon

Marriage, Sexuality, and Contraception: Natural Law,
Moral Discernment, and the Authority
of the Church 86
Jean Porter

Conscience and Contraception: Telling Our Stories—
Natural Family Planning: Sharing the Struggles 92
Rachel Espinoza and Tawny Horner

Conscience and Contraception: Telling Our Stories—
My Mother's Burden 96
Olive Barnes

Conscience and Contraception: Telling Our Stories—
Vatican Roulette...99
Amelia Beck

Conscience and Contraception: Telling Our Stories—
Wanting a Different Life...101
Giovanna Solari-Masson

Conscience and Contraception: Telling Our Stories—
A "Millennial's" Perspective.....................................103
Emma Jane Harris

Same-Sex Marriage and the Catholic Community.................106
Margaret A. Farley

Same-Sex Love: Telling Our Stories—Living under the
Radar, or Celebrating Family in All Its Forms? 110
Sophie Stanes and Deborah Woodman

Same-Sex Love: Telling Our Stories—"The Glory of
God Is a Human Being Fully Alive" 113
Ursula Halligan

Same-Sex Love: Telling Our Stories—Getting Hooked:
Being Lesbian and Becoming Catholic 116
Eve Tushnet

Being Good and Doing Bad? Virtue Ethics and
Sexual Orientation 120
Katie Grimes

"What's Love Got to Do with It?" Women's
Experience of Celibacy...124
Janette Gray

Singled Out: The Vocation to Solitude 128
Patricia Stoat

PART THREE—
Poverty, Exclusion, and Marginalization **131**

Introduction to Part Three 133

"A Mysticism of Open Eyes": Catholic Women's Voices
from a Marginal Neighborhood of Buenos Aires 137
Ana Lourdes Suárez and Gabriela Zengarini

Challenging Families: Indian Women Speak
from the Margins...141
Astrid Lobo Gajiwala

Reading the Signs of the Times: Maternal Mortality
and Reproductive Rights...146
Nontando Hadebe

Maternal Migration and Paternal Responsibility in the
Philippines: Challenges for the Church 150
Agnes M. Brazal

Contents

PART FOUR—
Institutions and Structures...**155**

Introduction to Part Four..157

Roles for Women in the Church...161
  Mary Aquin O'Neill

Breathing with Only One Lung: Where Are the
  Women's Voices in the Synods? 164
  Lucetta Scaraffia

It's Not All about Eve: Women in the Lectionary..................168
  Christine Schenk

"The Apostle to the Apostles": Women Preaching
  the Good News 172
  Madeleine Fredell

Young Catholic Women Working in Ministry:
  Blessings, Challenges, and Hopes......................................175
  Rhonda Miska

On Elephants, Angels, and Trust: The Structure
  of the Church and Catholic Families 179
  Catherine Cavanagh

Epilogue 183
  Editorial Team

FOREWORD

Of Listening Ears and Prophetic Voices

AGBONKHIANMEGHE OROBATOR, SJ

Nigerian theologian Elochukwu Uzukwu's endearing image of "a listening church" or "church with large ears"[1] evokes Pope Francis's ecclesiological vision of compassion and mercy as defining marks of the Church. Listening with large ears is a constitutive feature of the African communicative ethics of palaver, a practice that allows the spoken word to make its rounds in the community untrammeled by narrow interests or ideological predilections. When understood in the context of palaver, Church becomes a space of dialogue and conversation, of speaking and listening, with courage and respect, honesty and humility. A listening church eschews the atavistic propensity to censor and silence voices, especially those echoing from the peripheries and margins of the community of believers.

Francis has returned to this theme of listening and dialogue as recently as his encyclical letter *Laudato Si'*. On matters concerning the care for our common home, the pope calls for honest and open debate that is respectful of divergent views; a broad, responsible, comprehensive, and courageous debate capable of "calling things by their names" (*LS* 135; cf. 188 and 201). His relentless call for debate and dialogue is refreshing not only for the Church's engagement in the global conversation on ecology, but also for the consistency, integrity, and credibility of its teaching and proclamation of the gospel of Jesus

Christ. Francis's appeal for debate and dialogue in *Laudato Si'* rhymes with his mantra on the universality of ecological and human relationality that he pithily renders as "everything is connected" and "everything is related" (*LS* 91, 92, 117, 240). Such cosmic relationality forswears exclusion and affirms the belief that "we human beings are united as brothers and sisters on a wonderful pilgrimage, woven together by the love God has for each of his creatures and which also unites us in fond affection with brother sun, sister moon, brother river and mother earth" (*LS* 92). In this pilgrimage of inclusion, sisters and brothers, mothers and fathers, together image the fundamental spiritual equality of all human beings.

Dialogue and debate constitute an arduous exercise. Oftentimes we are tempted to mitigate, even eliminate, the concomitant tension and friction by preselecting our conversation partners or screening out those voices that we do not want to hear or whose opinions we argue against and disagree with. To succumb to this temptation is to undermine the credibility of the exercise. Authentic dialogue and debate embrace difference and affirm the equality and dignity of all conversation partners no matter their situation. There are no outsiders or insiders.

In the spirit of Pope Francis's call for dialogue and debate about the issues that matter in Church and society, this anthology edited by the Catholic Women Speak Network assembles voices of women from across the globe. Each voice is unique, not a collective. In life a voice is not a disembodied or disincarnate reality. A voice is a carrier of narratives and bearer of multiple experiences birthed and lived in a variety of contexts. In every voice there is a story. And every story is unique. The narratives voiced by contributors to this anthology are at times joyful and jolting, consoling and painful, exhilarating and exasperating. They tell of "the joys and hopes, the griefs and anxieties" that Catholic women live and experience in multiple forms of human sexuality, family, marriage, and relationships. They lament the painful exclusion, violence, and poverty that compound these experiences, and question the institutions and structures that sustain them, but without abandoning faith and hope—that each story will be heard, received, and affirmed with compassion, mercy, and humility. These virtues are constitutive of the self-understanding of the Church in the vision of Pope Francis, for whom the Church is a community that "has an endless desire to show mercy" and "is a place of mercy freely given, where everyone can feel welcomed, loved and encouraged to live the good life of the Gospel" (*EG* 24, 114; see 37).

A prayerful reading of these narratives allows us to appreciate the complexity and depth of the human condition when it comes to the understanding and practice of relationship in all its varied forms. There is no pretension to perfection. It is a zone of imperfection, flaws, and limitations not uncharacteristic of the essence of humanity. Happily the gospel unequivocally proclaims that the gap between divine perfection and human limitation constitutes a powerful rationale for the mystery of the incarnation (see Mark 2:17). This gospel truth transforms the Church into a place of compassionate listening and prophetic action.

Intended as a contribution to the synodal process of the Fourteenth Ordinary General Assembly of the Synod of Bishops on the family, this anthology gathers voices from the byways and highways, from the altar of ecclesial ministries and pews, from academia and public square, center and periphery, to create a richly variegated resource for all who are concerned about understanding and actualizing "The Vocation and Mission of the Family in the Church and Contemporary World." Listening to the voices represented in this collection of essays calls for grace to make room for difference, diversity, and divergence, and to recognize the spiritual and prophetic impulses that drive the narratives. There is a difference between Babel and Pentecost. The former breeds confusion and chaos, the latter understanding and harmony. Neither is an easy experience to manage. The voices in this anthology enrich and expand the banquet of ecclesial conversation with assorted gifts worthy of a new Pentecost. It is of the nature of the Spirit of the risen Christ to empower disciples with courage in the proclamation of the truth. Similarly, it is a healthy mark of the Church to be able to listen with joy and gratitude to what each voice brings to the table (see *LS* 155).

As mentioned, the experiences narrated by the voices in this anthology are painful and joyful, and the hurts and struggles run deep. They mirror the life of the body of Christ that elects to inhabit the "messy" spaces of the margins and the peripheries of human existence. Pope Francis has challenged the Church to embrace these realities with courage and boldness, lest we become like the infantile generation denounced by Jesus of Nazareth for foolishly ridiculing the in-breaking of the reign of God and thus becoming incapable of rejoicing with the piper or reciting dirges with the mourners, preferring instead to loaf in the placid square of self-referential and self-interested orthodoxy.

Compiled with a view to the 2015 Synod on the Family, this anthology reminds us that treating half the members of the body of Christ as outsiders or assigning them second-class status is a detritus of history and tradition unsuited for the twenty-first century and unfounded in the gospel. The exclusion of the majority in deciding the teachings and affairs of the body of Christ seems like a distortion and mutilation of this body. To remedy such malady, Francis advocates a spirituality of inclusion and solidarity flowing "from the mystery of the Trinity" and engendering a reconciled, liberated, and wholesome humanity and community called Church (*LS* 240). This anthology echoes this spirituality.

To return to the virtue of ecclesial listening. Depending on where we stand on the doctrinal spectrum, what we hear in this anthology may delight or discomfit us. Whatever our position or reaction, may we draw confidence and fortitude from Pope Francis's assertion that "God is not afraid of new things! That is why he is continually surprising us, opening our hearts, and guiding us in unexpected ways."[2] This anthology offers the body of Christ an opportunity to encounter the God of surprises with open hearts in unexpected ways.

NOTES

1. Elochukwu Uzukwu, *A Listening Church: Autonomy and Communion in African Churches* (Maryknoll, NY: Orbis Books, 1996).

2. Pope Francis, homily at the beatification of Pope Paul VI (October 19, 2014), http://www.zenit.org/en/articles/pope-s-hom ily-at-the-beatification-mass-of-paul-vi.

PREFACE

The Catholic Women Speak Network is an online forum for theological dialogue and collaboration among women about issues relating to their participation, presence, and representation in society and the Church. It has more than seven hundred members drawn from across the world communicating primarily through social media. Many of them are connected to wider networks of academic theologians, pastoral workers, and educators. The highly effective channels of communication provided by the Network made it possible to compile this book in a very short space of time (eight weeks in all), bringing together a range of contributors to produce an anthology of Catholic women's writings in advance of the 2015 Synod of Bishops on the Vocation and Mission of the Family in the Church and Contemporary World.

A team of editors, translators, and readers collaborated to produce the final manuscript, but the book would not have been possible without the willing cooperation and encouragement of all the contributors. The editorial team included Anne Arabome, Tina Beattie, Diana Culbertson, Séverine Deneulin, Cristina Lledo Gomez, and Susan O'Brien, with valuable assistance in translation and proofreading provided by Olive Barnes, Rhonda Miska, Rebecca Bratten Weiss, and Chiara Brown. We owe a particular debt of gratitude to Paulist Press for being willing to publish this at very short notice, with special thanks to Trace Murphy for his commitment, advice and hard work in bringing the project to completion.

For further reading, resources, and links to longer versions of some of the essays published here, please visit the Catholic Women Speak Network at http://www.catholicwomenspeak.com/.

CONTRIBUTORS

Anne Arabome, SSS, originally from Nigeria, is a member of the Sisters of Social Service in Los Angeles, California. She holds a doctor of ministry degree in spirituality from Catholic Theological Union in Chicago and is working on a doctorate in systematic theology at the University of Roehampton, London.

Olive Barnes was born and raised in rural Ireland to devout Catholic parents. She moved to England for work and returned to postgraduate study after raising her children. She has been a eucharistic minister; reader; catechist for first holy communion, confirmation, and RCIA, and a Catholic school governor.

Tina Beattie is professor of Catholic studies at the University of Roehampton in London. She has published in the areas of Marian theology, gender and sacramentality, and theology and human rights. She is a past president of the Catholic Theological Association of Great Britain and a member of Cafod's theological advisory group. She converted to Catholicism in 1986 at the age of thirty-one. She and her husband have four children and a grandson.

Amelia Beck is an English woman who converted from Anglicanism to Catholicism at age eighteen, and married a Catholic Irishman when she was twenty. She is now in her seventies. ("Amelia Beck" is a *nom de plume*).

Pippa Bonner is a retired social worker, latterly running a hospice bereavement service. In her forties she completed a master's in theology and religious studies. Now she babysits her grandchildren, writes, is part of a collaborative parish, and volunteers in her local hospital chaplaincy team.

Agnes M. Brazal is professor at the St. Vincent School of Theology, Adamson University, Philippines, and founding member and former president of the Catholic Theological Society of the Philippines (DaKaTeo). She is author, coauthor, or coeditor of five books, a textbook series, and essays on Filipino/Asian/migration/cyber theologies and ethics.

Lisa Sowle Cahill, PhD, University of Chicago, is the Monan Professor of Theology at Boston College. She is past president of the Catholic Theological Society of America and the Society of Christian Ethics. Her works include *Global Justice, Christology and Christian Ethics; Theological Bioethics*, and *Sex, Gender and Christian Ethics*. She and her husband are the parents of five children.

Anna Cannon is a Polish cradle Catholic in her late sixties, living in England and the mother of one daughter. She is a qualified medical herbalist, which is her vocation and ministry. Hildegard of Bingen is her patron and Ecclesiasticus 38:4 is her motto: "The Lord created medicines out of the earth, and the sensible will not despise them."

Catherine Cavanagh is a lifelong Catholic and a candidate in the doctor of ministry program at Regis College, University of Toronto. She works as a teacher and high school chaplain within the publicly funded Catholic school system of Ontario, Canada.

Julie Clague lectures in Christian theology and ethics at the University of Glasgow and researches in the field of moral theology. In 2014, she edited a special issue of the *Heythrop Journal* on "Faith, Family and Fertility," dealing with topics of relevance for the Synod on the Family and for Catholic engagement with the United Nations sustainable development goals. She edits the European forum of Catholic theological ethics in the World Church (www.catholicethics. com).

Rachel Espinoza has a master's of divinity degree from the University of Notre Dame and is a parish pastoral associate in Chicago; **Tawny Horner** is a mother of three in Falls Church, Virginia. They met through online communities for practitioners of Natural Family Planning.

Margaret A. Farley is Professor Emerita of Christian Ethics at Yale Divinity School. She is the author or coeditor of eight books, including *Personal Commitments*, *Just Love*, and *Changing the Questions*, as well as many essays on issues in theological and philosophical ethics. She is past president of the Society of Christian Ethics and the Catholic Theological Society of America.

Madeleine Fredell, OP, has degrees in Latin, French, and general linguistics; in teaching, and in biblical studies, Greek, and Hebrew from *Institut Catholique* in Paris. She has an MA in contemporary theology from Heythrop College, University of London. She is secretary general of the Swedish Justice and Peace Commission and is presently prioress of the Swedish vicariate of Saint Dominic's Roman Congregation.

Astrid Lobo Gajiwala established India's first Tissue Bank, and was the first woman President of the Asia-Pacific Association of Tissue Banks. A member of Indian and Asian theological associations, she has been published widely. She has been a consultant for the Indian bishops since 1992 and helped draft their gender policy. She is a partner in an interfaith marriage.

Cristina Lledo Gomez has a PhD in theology from Charles Sturt University, Australia. Her thesis was titled "Mother Church as Metaphor in the Vatican II Documents." For the 2015–2016 academic year, she is a visiting research fellow at Boston College's School of Theology and Ministry. Cristina is a Filipina native but lives in Australia with her husband and two children.

Janette Gray, RSM, is lecturer in systematic theology at the Yarra Theological Union within the University of Divinity, Melbourne, Australia. She received a PhD from Cambridge University and has lectured in the United Kingdom, United States, Philippines, and New Zealand.

Katie Grimes is an assistant professor of theology at Villanova University. She studies racism, just war theory, and sexual ethics. She was born and raised in Marion, Ohio, and writes for the blog *Women in Theology*.

Nontando Hadebe is currently a Fulbright Scholar at Emmanuel College in Boston, and prior to this was an international fellow at the Jesuit School of Theology, Santa Clara University. She completed her doctorate at St. Augustine College, South Africa, where she teaches pastoral and systematic theology. She is a member of the Circle of African women theologians.

Ursula Halligan is political editor of TV3, Ireland's commercial television station. She was educated at Our Lady's Secondary School, Templeogue, Dublin (run by the Religious of Christian Education) and later at University College Dublin where she graduated with an honors BA degree in history and politics and an MA in politics.

Emma Jane Harris is a twenty-four-year-old postgraduate student and research assistant at the Margaret Beaufort Institute of Theology, Cambridge in England. She has studied theology in Bristol and Paris. Her research interests lie in post–Vatican II theology and contemporary gender theory.

Elizabeth Johnson, PhD, CSJ, is Distinguished Professor of Theology at Fordham University in New York City. Her writings have been translated into thirteen languages. She has served on the Lutheran-Catholic Dialogue (United States), the US Bishops' Committee on Women in Church and Society, and Common Ground Initiative started by Cardinal Joseph Bernardin (Chicago) to reconcile polarized groups in the Church. She is past president of the Catholic Theological Society of America and the ecumenical American Theological Society.

Alison Concannon Kennedy is cofounder and CEO of the Watermead Music and Publishing Apostolate. She is a parish and diocesan musician, and a composer of liturgical music and many hymns. For the past fifteen years she has been working as a pastoral assistant in a busy city parish in Leicester, England.

Ursula King, STL (Paris), MA (Delhi), PhD (London), FRSA, is Professor Emerita of Theology and Religious Studies, University of Bristol, England. Educated in Germany, France, India, and England, she has lectured all over the world, published widely and holds honorary doctorates from the Universities of Edinburgh (1996), Oslo (2000), and Dayton/Ohio (2003). Married for over fifty years, she and her husband have four daughters and six grandchildren.

Trish Madigan, OP, is currently the director of the Dominican Centre for Interfaith Ministry, Education and Research in Sydney, Australia. Before that she spent over fifteen years as the director of the Catholic Church's office of ecumenical and interfaith relations in Sydney. She has a doctorate in Arabic and Islamic studies and has written extensively on the lives of Muslim and Catholic women.

Sara Maitland studied English at Oxford University where she discovered feminism, socialism, Christianity, and friend-ship—the bedrock of her adult life. She was received into the Catholic Church in 1994 at the age of forty-four. In 2006 she moved to an isolated moor in South West Scotland to explore a life of silence and solitude. She writes both fiction and nonfiction.

Cettina Militello, PhD, STD, is associate professor at the Pontifical Institute of Sacred Liturgy in Rome and directs the Constanza Scelfo Institute for problems of the laity and women in the Church (Department of the Italian Society for Theological Research). She holds the Chair of Woman and Christianity at the Pontifical Theological Faculty Marianum. Her academic interests include ecclesiology, Mariology, women in the Church, and the relationship between ecclesiology and liturgy.

Rhonda Miska is a lay ecclesial minister, freelance writer, for-mer Jesuit Volunteer, and graduate of the Boston College School of Theology and Ministry. Her past ministries include coordinating parish Hispanic and social justice ministries, leading returned missioner reentry retreats, and serving as campus minister. She is now based at a retreat center in Iowa.

Mary Aquin O'Neill is a Sister of Mercy with a doctorate in reli-gion from Vanderbilt University. After many years of college teaching, she founded Mount Saint Agnes Theological Center for Women in Baltimore, Maryland, and was its director from

1992 to 2009. Since the Center closed in August of 2013, she is in semiretirement, writing as well as giving lectures and retreats.

Jean Porter is the John A. O'Brien Professor of Moral Theology at the University of Notre Dame, Indiana, where she has taught for twenty-five years. She is the author of five books and numerous articles on natural law, Thomistic ethics, and related subjects. Her current project is a study of justice considered as a personal virtue.

Carolina del Río has a master's in fundamental theology from the Pontifical Catholic University of Chile. She is a journalist and licensed in Social Sciences and Information, and she teaches at the Santa Maria Spirituality Center. She is a member of the "Study Circle of Sexuality and the Gospel" at the Manuel Larrain Theological Center, and a participant in Argentina's "Teologanda" program of study, research, and publications. She is the author of *La Irrupción de los Laicos*, with María Olga Delpiano (Santiago: Editorial Uqbar, 2011), and *Quien Soy Yo Para Juzgar, testimonios de homosexuales católicos* (Santiago: Editorial Uqbar, 2015).She has four children.

Lucetta Scaraffia is an Italian historian with a special interest in stories of women and Christianity. She is a member of the National Committee on Bioethics and of the Pontifical Council for the New Evangelization. She has published several books and contributes to numerous journals, including *l'Osservatore Romano*, for which she edits the monthly column, *Donne, Chiesa, Mondo*.

Christine Schenk is an American sister of the Congregation of St. Joseph and a regular contributor to the *National Catholic Reporter*. Previously she worked as a nurse midwife serving low-income Cleveland families. Schenk holds master's degrees in nursing and theology from Boston College and Cleveland St. Mary Seminary, respectively. She is a cofounder of FutureChurch, an international coalition working for full participation of all Catholics in church life and leadership. She retired from the organization in 2013.

Giovanna Solari-Masson is from an Italian Catholic family. She lives in London and is married with two young daughters. She and her husband run a business together. Her voluntary activities include South London Citizens, *Pax Christi*, and Brixton Justice and Peace. She supports the Brixton and Norwood food bank and campaigns for the living wage.

Janet Martin Soskice is Professor of Philosophical Theology at the University of Cambridge and president of Jesus College. A mother of two daughters, she is a past president of the Catholic Theological Association of Great Britain and the Society for the Study of Theology. Her works include *The Kindness of God* (OUP, 2008) and *Sisters of Sinai* (Chatto and Knopf, 2009), which was chosen for the "Best Books of the Year" lists of the *Christian Science Monitor* and the *Washington Post.*

Sophie Stanes and Deborah Woodman are two London-based lifelong Catholics, six years into their civil partnership. Sophie is a photographer and also works for a religious order. Deborah is a clinical psychologist in the National Health Service.

Patricia Stoat is a retired librarian, single, and a contemporary urban hermit living in England. She has been an atheist, a Buddhist, and finally came home to the Catholic Church. She is passionate about justice and peace, and the development of interreligious dialogue. She chairs the Nottingham Diocese Justice and Peace Commission.

Ana Lourdes Suárez is professor and researcher at the Pontifical Catholic University of Argentina in Buenos Aires. She has a PhD in sociology from the University of California, San Diego, and a PhD in anthropology from the University of Buenos Aires. She coordinates the Interdisciplinary Program, "The Religious Presence in Buenos Aires Slums," and she participates in Argentina's "Teologanda" program of study, research, and publications.

Eve Tushnet is the author of *Gay and Catholic: Accepting My Sexuality, Finding Community, Living My Faith* (Ave Maria: 2014). She entered the Catholic Church in 1998 and is a

writer in Washington, DC. She blogs at http://www.patheos.
com/blogs/evetushnet/.

Clare Watkins is a Catholic theologian who has juggled theological work in ecclesiology, sacramental theology, and practical theology with married life and the raising of four children. She teaches at the University of Roehampton, London, and is currently chair of the British and Irish Association for Practical Theology.

Margaret Watson is a Catholic convert, married to a Baptist for over forty years. Now retired and living in Britain, she was previously a nurse and midwife and then ordained as a Salvation Army Officer.

Gabriela Zengarini, OP, is Professor of Religious Studies at the Northern University of St. Thomas, Haedo, Buenos Aires. She is a Dominican Sister of the Most Holy Name of Jesus. She holds a master's in dogmatic theology with specialization in missiology from the Faculty of Theology, *Nossa Senhora da Assunção*, São Paulo. She shares her life and mission in the community of the *barrio* Carlos Gardel in Greater Buenos Aires.

INTRODUCTION

In his opening address to the 2014 Extraordinary General Assembly of the Synod of Bishops, Pope Francis reminded his fellow bishops of their "great responsibility: to carry the realities and the problems of the Churches, to help them walk on that path that is the Gospel of the family." He encouraged them to speak with *parrhesia*—"to say all that, in the Lord, one feels the need to say: without polite deference, without hesitation."[1] Even though few women were present when he gave his address, the contributors to this book have taken Pope Francis at his word and have spoken with *parrhesia*.

This anthology is a collaboration among many women who believe that the Church cannot come to a wise and informed understanding of family life without listening to women. Cardinal Ravasi, president of the Pontifical Council for Culture, in a letter sending his greetings to the contributors, described the book as "a narrative enchiridion of some of the issues—or rather persons—whose voices are an essential part of our community." He expressed his "commitment to listen to every voice and to have free and serious dialogue, even on delicate and complex questions, with people who believe, with those who do not believe, and with those who believe or think differently."[2] We hope and pray that other leaders in the Church will be equally open to dialogue, so that this book might be a resource for all who are responsible for the Church's ministry to families in the modern world, and for those who wish to understand how women's lives are shaped by their faith in Christ and the teachings of the Church.

Contributors to the book represent a little of the rich diversity and complexity of Catholic women's lives, not only as wives and mothers but as women who are single, women in religious life, professional women, single mothers, women without children, divorced and remarried women, lesbian women, academic theologians, and women in a wide range of pastoral, social, and domestic roles. We are Catholic women who practice our faith and seek prayerfully to understand and respect the Church's teachings. We sometimes have difficulty, however, with the ways in which these teachings are interpreted and implemented through the Church's hierarchy and institutions, not least because these institutions remain overwhelmingly androcentric.

We are different in our cultures and contexts, and in our struggles and insights. We do not speak as one voice but as many voices with a common desire to enrich the Church through our differences, as we seek "a unity which is never uniformity but a multifaceted and inviting harmony" (*EG* 117). We believe that we have something to say that is not being heard when members of the hierarchy discuss women and family life. Apart from the roles that define us in relation to our families, we women remain "other" with regard to the Church's institutions and teachings. We are spoken about in language that seems remote and detached from our own endeavors to articulate "the joys and the hopes, the griefs and the anxieties of the women of this age, especially those who are poor or in any way afflicted" (*GS* 1).

We hope that the voices in this anthology will enrich the conversation. We are not all saying the same thing, however. We do not all share the same perspectives, and we do not all agree with one another. We do not speak as "Woman" but as many women who together form part of the body of Christ.

Our intention is to ask questions and explore issues that do not find space for open discussion in the Church. For example, while there were a few women present at the 2014 synod of bishops, most of them were invited to attend only in their capacity as wives, speaking with their husbands as couples who celebrate and uphold the Church's teaching on the family. While we value and respect their witness, we regret that no one spoke on behalf of the millions of Catholic women who do not so easily conform to this model. Despite the theme of the synod, those gathered did not engage with the work of women theologians who have for many years been writing on issues of marriage, family life, sexuality, and human relationships. In other words, women's voices were not heard in a way that would authentically represent the vast diversity of Catholic women's lives, nor was the contribution of women theologians acknowledged. In this book, we speak as some of those missing voices.

We are aware that no book can claim to encapsulate the vast diversity of Catholic women's lives. However, we hope that our desire to open up a space of dialogue and encounter will enable others to speak and be heard. Pope Francis cautions against "imposing a monolithic uniformity" on our human diversity. He writes, "Differences between persons and communities can sometimes prove uncomfortable, but the Holy Spirit, who is the source of that diversity, can bring forth something good from all things and turn it into an attractive means of evangelization" (*EG* 131). We intend this book to be a means of evangelization—not in spite of but because of—the different points of view it represents. We acknowledge that some of these points of view might be uncomfortable perspectives to consider.

Pope Francis has said that "we have not yet come up with a profound theology of womanhood, in the Church."[3] Such comments reduce women to objects of study, a separate category of reflection. Theology, from this perspective, is primarily for and about men—the *we* implicitly referred to here. Women have been doing theology since the time of the New Testament. Indeed, one could argue that the first Christology was articulated by pregnant women, when Elizabeth, "filled with the Holy Spirit," recognized Mary as "the mother of my Lord" (Luke 1:41, 43).

We resist, therefore, any suggestion that the Church needs a theology of "Woman" or "womanhood." Rather than a deeper theology of women, we say that the Church needs a deeper theology of the human—a theological anthropology that can be developed only by the full inclusion of women in the process of theological reflection informed by the experiential realities of daily life. In her welcoming address to participants at a conference on "Women in the Church: Prospects for Dialogue" at the Pontifical Antonianum University in April 2015, the university's rector, Sister Mary Melone, said, "We are not mere guests—we are the Church, and we wish to be so more intensely." That is the spirit in which this book has been written.

Pope Francis speaks of the need for us to become a "messy" Church, a Church that is not afraid to take risks in order to live the joyous adventure of faith. This book expresses the messy realities of women's lives, realities that challenge the Church's current practice in many ways, realities that the Church must acknowledge in order to communicate the joy of the gospel to future generations. In *Evangelii Gaudium*, Pope Francis quotes St. Thomas Aquinas, who in turn cites St. Augustine, to argue that "the precepts which Christ and the apostles gave to the people of God 'are very few'" (*EG* 43).[4] This means, says Pope Francis, that

> the precepts subsequently enjoined by the Church should be insisted upon with moderation "so as not to burden the lives of the faithful" and make our religion a form of servitude, whereas "God's mercy has willed that we should be free."[5] This warning, issued many centuries ago, is most timely today. It ought to be one of the criteria to be taken into account in considering a reform of the Church and her preaching which would enable it to reach everyone. (*EG* 43)

This book tells of the burdens that women bear in a tradition that too often continues to make religion a form of female servitude. It also tells stories of courage and joy, patience and perseverance, often in the face of extreme adversity. The chapters constitute a chorus of women's voices speaking of faith, hope, and love, without fear and without self-censorship. We hope that those reading these pages will "listen with humility"[6] to what their sisters say, in order that dialogue can begin.

We have ensured that all the pieces are relatively short and accessible to a general readership.[7] This editorial decision allows us to disclose the rich diversity, engagement, and learning of Catholic women today. The hierarchy has not acknowledged this diversity because it speaks about us but seldom with us. Meanwhile, secular culture often dismisses Catholic women as subservient handmaids in a Church that is perceived as patriarchal. This book suggests that these impoverished attitudes do not do justice to our faith in Christ, our fidelity to the Church, and our considered reasons for remaining Catholic. Beyond all the inevitable frustrations and failings of our finite institutions and fallible lives, we discover in the Scriptures, mediated through the faith and sacraments of the Catholic Church, our communal home on earth and our hope of that eternal joy where we shall all share as beloved of Christ in the heavenly wedding feast.

The Catholic Women Speak Network
July 2015

NOTES

1. Pope Francis, "Greeting to the Synod Fathers during the First General Congregation of the Third Extraordinary General Assembly of the Synod of Bishops," Monday, October 6, 2014, https://w2.vatican.va/content/francesco/en/speeches/2014/october/documents/papa-francesco_20141006_padri-sinodali.html.

2. Gianfranco Cardinal Ravasi, president, Pontifical Council for Culture, personal letter to Tina Beattie, July 7, 2015. Quoted with permission from Cardinal Ravasi.

3. "Press Conference of Pope Francis during the Return Flight, Apostolic Journey to Rio de Janeiro on the Occasion of the XXVIII World Youth Day, Papal flight, Sunday, July 28, 2013," at https://w2.vatican.va/content/francesco/en/speeches/2013/july/documents/papa-francesco_20130728_gmg-conferenza-stampa.html, accessed July 22, 2015.

4. Citing *S. Th.*, *I-II*, q. 107, a. 4.

5. Ibid.

6. Pope Francis, "Greeting to the Synod Fathers."

7. Links to longer versions of some of the articles are available on our website, as well as other articles and links for those who want to read further. Please go to http://www.catholicwomen speak.com/.

ABBREVIATIONS USED IN REFERENCES TO CHURCH DOCUMENTS

(These are all available to download from the Vatican website: http://w2.vatican.va/content/vatican/en.html.)

RN Pope Leo XIII, "Encyclical on Capital and Labor" (*Rerum Novarum*), May 15, 1891.

QA Pope Pius XI, "Encyclical on Reconstruction of the Social Order" (*Quadragesimo Anno*), May 15, 1931.

PT Pope John XXIII, "Encyclical on Establishing Universal Peace in Truth, Justice, Charity, and Liberty" (*Pacem in Terris*), April 11, 1963.

LG Pope Paul VI, "Dogmatic Constitution on the Church" (*Lumen Gentium*), November 21, 1964.

GE Pope Paul VI, "Declaration on Christian Education" (*Gravissimum Educationis*), October 28, 1965.

GS Pope Paul VI, "Pastoral Constitution on the Church in the Modern World" (*Gaudium et Spes*), December 7, 1965.

OA Pope Paul VI, "Apostolic Letter on the Occasion of the Eightieth Anniversary of the Encyclical *Rerum Novarum*" (*Octogesima Adveniens*), May 14, 1971.

II Sacred Congregation for the Doctrine of the Faith, "Declaration on the Question of Admission of Women to the Ministerial Priesthood" (*Inter Insigniores*), October 15, 1976.

LE Pope John Paul II, "Encyclical On Human Work" (*Laborem Exercens*), September 14, 1981.

FC Pope John Paul II, "Apostolic Exhortation on the Role of the Christian Family in the Modern World" (*Familiaris Consortio*), November 22, 1981.

MD Pope John Paul II, "Apostolic Letter On the Dignity and Vocation of Women" (*Mulieris Dignitatem*), August 15, 1988.

CCC Catechism of the Catholic Church, Libreria Editrice Vaticana, Citta del Vaticano 1993.

OS Pope John Paul II, "Apostolic Letter on Reserving Priestly Ordination to Men Alone" (*Ordinatio Sacerdotalis*), May 22, 1994.

EG Pope Francis, "Apostolic Exhortation on the Proclamation of the Gospel in Today's World" (*Evangelii Gaudium*), November 24, 2013.

PD III Extraordinary General Assembly, "Pastoral Challenges to the Family in the Context of Evangelization" Preparatory Document (Vatican City, 2013).

IL III Extraordinary General Assembly, "The Pastoral Challenges of the Family in the Context of Evangelization" (*Instrumentum Laboris*) (Vatican City, 2014).

Lin. XIV Ordinary General Assembly, "The Vocation and Mission of the Family in the Church and Contemporary World" (*Lineamenta*) (Vatican City, 2014).

SF International Theological Commission, "*Sensus Fidei* in the Life of the Church" (Vatican City, 2014).

LS Pope Francis, "Encyclical Letter on Care for our Common Home" (*Laudato Si'*), May 24, 2015.

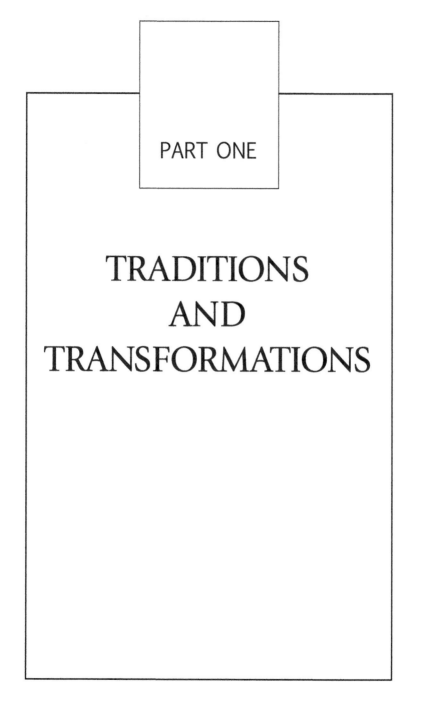

PART ONE

TRADITIONS
AND
TRANSFORMATIONS

INTRODUCTION
TO PART ONE

The last half century has seen a global revolution in the self-understanding of women, a dramatic change that poses many challenges to historical institutions, cultures, and religions. The Catholic Church has played a major role in the empowerment of women through education, and it remains a major provider of education and health care to poor women and girls. Nevertheless, women are still subordinate to men in all the Church's institutions and structures. The contributors in part 1 consider some of the ways in which women who engage with the Church's theological and biblical traditions are questioning existing paradigms of Catholic thought and practice.

Cettina Militello offers a broad overview of women in the Bible and the history of the Church, then examining how the Church since Vatican II has responded to the changing roles and expectations of women in Western society. She argues that Christian baptism is a sacrament of initiation that is identical for both sexes. This theological reality calls for full and equal participation of women in recognition of "the new awareness that God's design is fully inclusive."

Ursula King explores the riches of the Catholic intellectual tradition in the context of her own theological development. She speaks of women "tearing down an invisible wall of silence" to discover an authentic theological voice as part of this "gloriously rich intellectual inheritance." Reflecting on her experience of studying theology in an academic environment consisting almost exclusively of men studying for the priesthood, she appeals for more resources to be made available for women to study and teach theology.

Janet Martin Soskice explores the complex question of sexual difference, from interpretations of the Book of Genesis to the theology of the conciliar and postconciliar Church. She suggests that the Trinity offers a way of understanding sexual difference as being "good in itself," because it expresses difference in terms of the "creativity, reciprocity and generation...of the creature made in the image of God."

Elizabeth Johnson reflects on the New Testament account of the encounter between Jesus and a woman bent double with infirmity (Luke 13:10–13), to offer a vision of the liberating love of Jesus for women. In the face of continuing inequalities, women theologians turn to the Jesus of the Gospels to discover a promise of liberation, consolation, and friendship, calling for a "conversion of hearts, minds, and structures so that the reign of God may take firmer hold in this world."

Anne Arabome also focuses on Jesus as a liberating figure for women, this time in the context of African women's lives. She points out that an African Christology is emerging so that "Jesus is now very present in Africa." However, in a Church where women's voices are still not heard and their struggles are still not fully acknowledged, the question remains: "Who is Christ for African women?"

From a different cultural perspective, Carolina del Río Mena explores the ambiguity of Mary in the lives of Latin American women in the context of machismo and *marianismo*. While Mary is a model of womanhood for many, for others she "has been the explosive source of deep rebellion and internal ruptures." Women theologians are recovering in Mary "the current and prophetic paradigm of a reconciled and actualized humanity," to create life-enhancing role models in the quest for justice and equality between the sexes.

Cristina Lledo Gomez also seeks to bring a more realistic model of motherhood into theological discourse, focusing on the motherhood of the Church. She argues that the image of Mother Church needs to reflect the realities of mothering in order to foster a more mature understanding of faith in the context of the maternal Church, in which all the people of God are called "to become mothers to others themselves."

Finally in this section, Trish Madigan describes how Catholic and Muslim women learn from one another in dialogue, discovering in their different religions sources of both exclusion and liberation. When women study their own traditions and scriptures—the Bible and the Qur'an—they encounter models of human flourishing that enable them to challenge established traditions and to seek the same opportunities within their religious worlds as are now offered in the secular world.

These essays offer fleeting but inspiring glimpses of the transformations taking place in many different Catholic cultures and contexts, as women move "from silence to speech, from invisibility to presence, from submission to co-responsibility" (Militello). They bear witness to the fact that the Church already has a wealth of women's theological reflections to draw upon as it seeks to develop a more inclusive and representative theology of what it means to be male and female, made in the image of God and bodily redeemed in Christ. This theological endeavor can only succeed if women theologians and biblical scholars are fully incorporated into the Church's process of theological reflection and doctrinal development.

WOMEN IN THE CHURCH

Models of the Past—
Challenges of Today

CETTINA MILITELLO
(TRANS. CHIARA D. BROWN, MA)

Today, the question of women is more important than ever, both in society and in the Church. Many inequalities between men and women have had, and continue to have, a religious basis—certainly specious, but one that weighs heavily on women's daily lives. Understanding the how and why of this inequality requires us to reinterpret the past and the present, allowing us to better discern and act.

MODELS OF THE PAST

The subjection of women is consistent with the cultures of the Old Testament, but there are some intruders into this perspective from a different way of thinking. Men and women are protagonists in a story of salvation, and human love becomes a symbol of God's covenant with his people. Yet this symbol projects the potential for the divine onto men and the limitations of creation onto women, thus establishing a relationship that is

This is an edited version of a paper given at a symposium on "Women in the Church: Perspectives in Dialogue" at the Pontifical University Antonianum, Rome on April 28, 2015.

unequal and imbalanced, socially and morally as well as religiously.

Jesus' community seems to have been different. His female disciples had a special relationship with him, free of all religious, political, and sexually based submission. The writers of Scripture mediated these relationships but inevitably overlaid them with their own anthropological/religious vision. While the oldest Pauline writings suggest the doing away of all discrimination (see Gal 3:28) and affirm the unique role played by women in the growth of the early Christian movement, by the time of the later Pauline writings the Church was already being assimilated into the patriarchal norms of the era.

Yet Christianity produced an innovation in the relationship between the sexes, in that Christian initiation is identical for men and women. The seal is baptism, and neither the gifts of the Holy Spirit nor participation in the blood and body of Jesus are differentiated by sex. However, this equality in the order of grace does not lead to similar social or legal equality. Women remain submissive in the order of history and thus excluded from all active religious, political, or moral agency.

In the face of a burgeoning feminism, the Church in the twentieth century tried to protect and preserve female distinctiveness by way of an all-out defense of the female stereotype. Given the cultural unsustainability of maintaining the disparity between men and women, this could be formulated as a shift from inequality to "unequal equality," in which the ultimate criterion of a well-ordered society remained the authority of the father or the husband.

However, women's awareness has begun to change. Their level of education has increased. The two world wars were a proving ground for their capacity to compensate for the absence of men in terms of production. In particular, the struggle for the right to vote was underway, which in the space of fifty years would see women in Europe becoming both electors and the elected. Women religious also participated in this emancipatory process, engaging in self-governance according to a female line of authority.

VATICAN II AND ITS RECEPTION

The most significant event in the recent history of Catholic women was the Second Vatican Council, the result of the prophetic vision of Pope John XXIII who, in his encyclical *Pacem in Terris* (*PT*) took women's access to public life as a "sign of the times" (*PT* 41). The Council did not open up a specific discussion on the question of women, but the documents explicitly condemn sexism in economic and social life (see *LG* 32; *GE* 1; *GS* 29, 60), and *Gaudium et Spes* in particular recognizes the importance of women in these spheres (see *GS* 9, 31, 34, 60). Finally, there is significant recognition of women's contribution to culture and its development (see *GE* 1, 8; *GS* 55, 60).

For women, the postconciliar period signaled access to the study, research, and teaching of theology. The acquisition of these tools only sharpened their demand for a more equal and meaningful presence in the Church, but this has not been without conflict and struggle.

The greatest point of contention has been women's exclusion from any liturgical ministry simply because they are women. *Inter Insigniores* (*II*), published in 1976, established the so-called iconic principle, which stated that only males could represent Christ in the priesthood. Females, on the contrary, could only represent the Church—even though the Church is actually made up of both men and women. *Inter Insigniores* had a devastating effect at a time when all Christian churches, except for Orthodox churches, were gradually opening up to a different resolution to the question of women's equality.

More than a decade later, Pope John Paul II again addressed the question of women, including ministry, in his 1988 apostolic letter, *Mulieris Dignitatem* (*MD*). He asserted the equal dignity of the human couple as a sign of intratrinitarian relatedness, of man and woman in the image of God constituting a *communio personarum*, an explicit sign of the *communio personarum in divinis* of which the human being is a dual expression. However, *Mulieris Dignitatem* simply reiterated the position of *Inter Insigniores* with regard to ministry.

In 1994, the admission of women to the ministry of the Anglican Church provoked another document, *Ordinatio Sacerdotalis* (*OS*). This confirmed the exclusion of women from ordained ministry, changing its theological status from a "disputed" matter to one that was "closed."

THE CHALLENGE: MUTUAL RECOGNITION

What many people are asking of the Church today is an attitude that is less dogmatic, more aware of the challenges that face us. A balanced, nonideological interpretation of the relationship between the sexes is not unimportant for the future of our communities. This attitude requires recognition of the prophetic dignity of women, who have never been excluded by reason of their sexual identity from receiving the gift of prophecy. Prophecy means discernment, critical capacity, and insightful interpretation of the present in order to envision the future—skills that women can and must exercise for the growth of the Christian community.

Women are the Church, in the fullness of baptismal, christic, and eucharistic law, which emanates from the sacrament of initiation. Limiting women to an inferior, marginal role is unacceptable. We must make space—much space—for their right and duty to participate.

Women have moved from silence to speech, from invisibility to presence, from submission to coresponsibility. The journey has been long and is far from complete, but the goal is now illuminated by the new awareness that God's design is fully inclusive. To stand face-to-face with one another, to experience reciprocity, generosity, mutual caretaking: this is the feeling of being in the world, in the concreteness of flesh that is marked and "redeemed," waiting to be transfigured.

THE CATHOLIC INTELLECTUAL TRADITION AND WOMEN THEOLOGIANS

URSULA KING

The Catholic community possesses a tremendous intellectual history and tradition marked by an intellectual endeavor and audacity that have often transformed histories and cultures. Such a precious inheritance is a great responsibility, for it must be cherished and handed down to future generations. This rich inheritance provides many resources for being a Catholic intellectual today, but it is also an ambiguous and often difficult heritage, which can only be passed on and appropriated with discernment.

SHARING MY PERSONAL STORY

As a Catholic woman academic, I now approach this intellectual tradition, initially such a strong component in the making of my personal identity, with a thoroughly questioning attitude, but also an attitude tinged with humility and still filled with love. It is rather like the experience with one's own parents when one wants to affirm close, loving bonds but is all

This is an edited extract from an essay published in Anthony J. Cernera and Oliver J. Morgan, eds., *Examining the Catholic Intellectual Tradition*, vol. 1 (Fairfield, CT: Sacred Heart University Press, 2000), 133–55. Published with permission.

11

too aware of the gaps, the shortcomings, the narrowness of vision, and limitations of achievement of another generation.

I was brought up in a traditionally Catholic rural area of Germany. My parents had settled in the city of Cologne, with its great Catholic tradition, but during the Second World War we were evacuated to a village near where my parents had originally come from. I spent most of my childhood there. My early education gave me a positive experience of a Catholic world I deeply loved and gave me a strong foundation for all subsequent learning.

Yet today I can also see that it was quite a narrow Catholic milieu, almost a kind of *Kulturkatholizismus*. Like millions of others, I simply took for granted the teachings of the Catholic faith, especially as I knew no other. Today I am a very different person and see many things differently, but I am still a member of the Catholic Church—a church I love, though this love now deeply hurts and even feels absurd at times.

As a young woman I experienced a vocation to study theology at university, though I did not come from an intellectual family at all. Everyone was a small businessman, a farmer, a skilled worker, or a tradesman. Note that these occupations are only those of men, for the women in our family were all housewives, and there was no tradition of learning or higher education for either women or men.

I was drawn by an intellectual vision and calling that proved stronger than all personal and financial obstacles, but as a student I was forever in a minority, often a minority of one. I was the permanent outsider among a large group of men studying theology and preparing for the priesthood. My critical faculties were not yet sufficiently developed to articulate the aim of becoming a Catholic woman intellectual or to see how this might be practically possible, nor was I critical enough to discern the oppressive structures of the educational system or question the male exclusiveness of the Catholic Church and its teaching authority. Yet I clearly remember an exhilarating sense of liberation when I heard a well-known woman professor of sociology lecturing with great authority at a Semaine des

Intellectuels Catholiques in Paris. After years of listening to male professors, I suddenly encountered a woman with whom I could identify, who unknowingly affirmed me in my own powers and determination to be a female teacher passionately concerned with intellectual issues. It was like tearing down an invisible wall of silence, piercing through an incapacitating muteness, and calling me into speech with words only found years later, and through many experiences of nonrecognition, refusal, and exclusion.

WOMEN AND THE CATHOLIC INTELLECTUAL TRADITION

Yet my personal experience is less important than the scale of refusal and exclusion experienced by all women in the Catholic Church every day. Will Catholic women ever be fully recognized? Will they be encouraged to make their full contribution to the intellectual life of the Church and, more importantly still, will women become real coequals and copartners in shaping the Catholic intellectual tradition? That is what will count in the end.

Now that an increasing number of women are taking up theology professionally and studying up to the highest levels of academic qualification, women have acquired the necessary theological tools to engage critically and constructively with the tradition. When examined from a critical gender perspective, many traditions of the Catholic Church can be seen to possess a profoundly ambiguous nature so that serious shortcomings in the acclaimed universality of the tradition are coming to light.

We women doubt the justice of the exclusive maleness of the institutional Church and challenge the hierarchy of its offices and functions that has enabled men to exercise their lordship over others rather than practice the ministry of service of which the gospel speaks. We women also doubt the traditional image of God, or rather the ambiguous and one-sided way in which it has been preached and transmitted so that it

13

has often performed an oppressive rather than a liberating function in the growth of human beings. Most of all we doubt whether Christian beliefs and the Church, as so often presented today, can remain credible in the light of contemporary experience, especially when one becomes aware of the frequently oppressive, exploitative, or paternalistic treatment of women.

Today, women are claiming a new, equal place in society and Church as full members in their own right with the opportunity to develop their full potential in every sphere of human life, and this includes the celebration of the powers of the intellect. For this, women need encouragement, but also concrete resources—time, space, money, access to education and training, job opportunities. Equal opportunities are needed for women not only to study theology, but also to teach it at all levels.

We possess a gloriously rich intellectual inheritance with the resources to respond creatively to change, but Catholics will have to wrestle with decisive challenges during this new millennium—the tradition cannot remain intact without some profound changes. Let us hope that the Catholic intellectual tradition will remain a truly living inheritance that continues to thrive, and to inspire women and men to work together in solidarity and community for a great human task and noble intellectual vocation. Only then will the Catholic tradition shine like a bright light in a new season.

IMAGO DEI: SEXUAL DIFFERENCE AND HUMAN BECOMING

JANET MARTIN SOSKICE

Christian anthropology is "eschatological": it understands our human nature not only in terms of what we are, but of what we may be. We have the potential to become what we are not yet, or are not fully.

Christian anthropology is close to theology not because we are so very God-like, but because we are created by God and our destiny—the destiny of all reasoning creatures, according to Aquinas—is to share in the life of God. Human beings are destined to become what they are not yet but they are also "godlike" in the sense that, in the words of Genesis, they are made in the image of God (Gen 1:26–27).

The Genesis text also speaks about sexual difference. It is constitutive of human beings, and it is good. However, unlike Genesis 1, where male and female together comprise the *imago*, Genesis 2 can be read as saying that Adam on his own was virtually sufficient. He could do everything, so it seems, except reproduce. Eve is made as a "helper," but "helper" was routinely understood by early theologians as a subordinate—leaping over the fact that elsewhere in Genesis God himself is described as "helper" using the same Hebrew word.

Extract from Janet Martin Soskice, "*Imago Dei*" in *The Kindness of God: Metaphor, Gender, and Religious Language* (Oxford: Oxford University Press), 35–51, originally published in *Concilium*, 2006/1: 35–41—reprinted with permission.

What kind of helper? Augustine famously surmised that for help in the fields another man would have been more useful, and for conversation another man more interesting. This, he concluded, leaves procreation as the one thing man cannot do by himself.

This picture of man (the male) as able to do everything except reproduce, has informed theological anthropology down to the modern period. It is, in its way, a kind of egalitarianism in which everyone is "Adam." Women bring nothing to the table but their reproductive capacity and "man" (here meaning "male") is the default position for humanity. This sexual monoculture is in one sense justifiable, for it rests on the conviction that women as well as men are fully in the image of God—a matter not uncontested in the early Church.

We find ourselves to this very day torn between two positions that are each compelling but seem at the same time incompatible. We must say that, christologically speaking, women and men cannot be different for "all will bear the image of the man of heaven" (1 Cor 15:49, translation altered). But we must also say that sexual difference is not, or should not be, a matter of theological indifference. Genesis 1 suggests that sexual difference has something to tell us, not just about human beings, but about God in whose image they are made, male and female. The unresolved question is—where, why, and how does sexual difference make a difference?

Sexual "monoculture" is evident in the otherwise quite revolutionary Vatican II document *Gaudium et Spes*. One of the striking features of *Gaudium et Spes* is its christocentric anthropology. It is a vision of the human being as everywhere related to Jesus Christ. The document was visionary in anticipating the changes taking place in the lives of women before feminism had made much of an impression in any of the Christian churches, but reading it now with a view to sexual difference is an interesting experience. Throughout the document "man" (*homo*) is meant to include everyone. At the heart of this document because, as it rightly insists, at the heart of the New Testament itself, is an anthropology in which "the mystery of man becomes clear only in the mystery of the incarnate Word. Adam, the first man (*primus homo*), was a type of the future, that is of Christ our Lord. Christ, the new Adam, in revealing the mystery of the Father and his love, makes man fully clear to himself, makes clear his high vocation" (GS 22).

The unanswered question is, "Does Christ make woman fully clear to herself?" What can it mean for women to say that "whoever follows Christ, the perfect man, himself becomes more of a man" (GS 4)? Is Christ the fulfilment of female "men" as well as male "men," and if so, how?

In contrast to *Gaudium et Spes* is the 2004 letter from the Congregation for the Doctrine of the Faith to Catholic bishops, "On the Collaboration of Men and Women in the Church and in the World."[1] Whereas *Gaudium et Spes* almost elides sexual difference, this speaks of sexual difference as "belonging onto-logically to creation," an expression that is hard to construe but that falls just short of saying that there is an "ontological dif-ference" between men and women. That would indeed be an odd claim, for one can see an ontological difference between a stone and a human being, but it would be difficult to see an ontological difference between a man and a woman, unless one also said there could be an *ontological* difference between any two individuals.

A more serious problem is theological. Too strong an insistence on ontological difference would make it impossible for women to say, in the words of *Gaudium et Spes*, that Christ "became truly one of us, like us in everything except sin." It is for this reason that we must insist that, christologically speak-ing, men and women *cannot* be different.

But is sexual difference then without theological impor-tance? Can we return to our tradition of sexual monoculture, of sexual "indifference"? I think not.

God is three in one, unity in difference. Human beings in their createdness mirror this divine procession of love in being more than one, male and female. We need to affirm that all human beings are the divine image, and that sexual difference has something to tell us about God and about ourselves. This is not that women were *made for men* any more (or any less) than men were *made for women*. The as-yet unsung glory of Genesis 1:26–27 is that the fullness of divine life and creativity is reflected by a human race that is male and female, which encompasses if not an ontological then a primal difference.

We become ourselves through being with others. They conceive and give birth to us, teach us to speak and to write. Whatever meaning we give it, the startling divine plural of Genesis 1:26, "Let us make humankind in our image, according to our likeness," is no accident. The Church fathers saw in it a reference to the Trinity. The point is not an androgynous God, or even a God who is both male and female. The point is rather difference, and from within difference creativity, reciprocity, and generation, not as of God, but as of the creature made in the image of God.

God is love. We learn love through the reciprocity of our human condition, through being in relation to others who are different from ourselves—mothers, fathers, brothers, husbands, and wives. Sexual difference is a template for the fruitfulness that can come not when two are the same, but when they are different. For human creatures, as for sea and dry land, light and dark, fecundity is in the interval. And this is why sexual difference is not just instrumental to marriage or even to the family. It is good in itself.

NOTE

1. Congregation for the Doctrine of the Faith, "Letter to the Bishops of the Catholic Church on the Collaboration of Men and Women in the Church and in the World," May 31, 2004, at http://www.vatican.va/roman_curia/congregations/cfaith/documents/rc_con_cfaith_doc_20040731_collaboration_en.html.

out, and his powerful words and healing touch bring strength to her twisted spine. "Woman, you are set free!"

Christian women today read this story as a revelation of what their relationship with Jesus can still bring about. Bent over by many forces, they find his powerful compassion a spur to liberation, enabling them to stand up straight. Women scholars are discovering that there are many scenes in the New Testament that show Jesus' love for women, his concern for their well-being, and his freeing effect on their lives, but over the centuries the power of these stories has often been ignored because the men who preach and teach usually do not appreciate the suffering that women bear.

Society: A recent United Nations report shows that, despite some advances in securing women's rights over the last twenty years, there are still significant gender inequalities in all societies. For example, "Globally, women's earnings are 24 percent less than men's," despite the fact that "in all regions women work more than men: they do almost two and a half times as much unpaid care and domestic work as men, and if paid and unpaid work are combined, women in almost all countries work longer hours than men each day."[1] Added to this, women and girls suffer in particular ways as a result of rising religious extremism, violent conflict, the global economic crisis, and the growing division between rich and poor. Women are subject to domestic violence at home, and are raped, prostituted, trafficked into sexual slavery, and murdered by men to a degree that is not reciprocal. Regarding education, employment, and other social goods, men have advantages simply by being born male. Racial and ethnic prejudices add further disadvantage to women, as does class privilege that disrespects women who are poor. Every culture has different dynamics, but it is always women who are regarded as of lesser value.

This situation, called *sexism*, or prejudice against women because of their sex, is rampant on a global scale. To point this out is to underscore statistics that make clear the struggles women face in society because of their gender. In no country on earth are women and men yet treated in an equal manner befitting their human dignity.

In 1995 the United Nations held a conference on women in Beijing, China. On that occasion Pope John Paul II wrote a *Letter to Women* strongly supporting the conference's agenda of social equality:

> As far as personal rights are concerned, there is an urgent need to achieve *real equality* in every area: equal pay for equal work, protection for working mothers, fairness in career advancements, equality of spouses with regard to family rights and the recognition of everything that is part of the rights and duties of citizens in a democratic State. This is matter of justice, but also of necessity.[2]

This was a most welcome letter, putting the Catholic Church squarely in league with women's struggle for justice. However, there are problems in the Church itself that the pope did not address.

Church: Christianity took shape in the culture of the Roman Empire where elite men held power over lesser men, women, children, and slaves. This social structure, called *patriarchy* (rule of the father), is a pyramid-shaped arrangement where power is always in the hands of the dominant man or men at the top. As the Church grew and became established, its leaders adopted this pattern for its own internal life. Within this system, women are of necessity placed in predetermined subordinate roles. Men teach and decide; women listen and obey.

The Church reflects this inequality in all of its aspects. Sacred texts, religious symbols, doctrines, moral teachings, canon laws, rituals, and governing offices are all designed and led by men. Even God is imagined most often as a powerful patriarch in heaven ruling the earth and its peoples. In turn, this sacred patriarchy justifies the rule of men over women in family and wider society. While the histories are different, a similar pattern afflicts all the world's religions.

In view of these burdens, women today are discovering how liberating an encounter with Jesus of the Gospels can be. His words to the first-century woman echo down through the centuries: "Woman, you are set free." A newly educated group of women theologians are exploring the meaning of this promise and the ways in which it might become reality. For two thousand years almost all Christian theology has been done by men. After the Second Vatican Council (1962–1965) opened the study of theology to laypersons in the Church, many women began to be educated in this field.

Theology in women's hands has discovered Jesus Christ as compassionate friend, liberator from burdens, consoling friend in sorrows, and ally of women's strivings. The blessing that women find in their relationship with Jesus is not simply private and spiritual, though it is certainly that. It affects their lives in public and social domains, inspiring the struggle for liberation from structures of domination in every dimension of life. In Christ's name, society and Church are called to conversion of hearts, minds, and structures so that the reign of God may take firmer hold in this world. This is a challenging view. But the liberating words have already been spoken: "Woman, you are set free from your ailment." Stand up.

NOTES

1. UN Women, Progress of the World's Women 2015–2016, "Transforming Economies, Realizing Rights," 2015, Executive Summary, available to download at http://progress.unwomen.org/en/2015/.

2. Pope John Paul II, "Letter to Women," June 29, 1995, https://w2.vatican.va/content/john-paul-ii/en/letters/1995/documents/hf_jp-ii_let_29061995_women.html.

WHO IS CHRIST FOR AFRICAN WOMEN?

ANNE ARABOME

Official narratives such as the first African Synod (1994) and the second African Synod (2009) wax eloquently about women constituting the backbone of the Church,[1] but in reality, women are the least recognized with regard to ministry and participation in leadership and decision making. There is a gap between rhetoric and practice with regard to the Catholic Church's teaching and the treatment of women in Africa. As I have observed elsewhere, "Following the call of the Second African Synod, African women are invited to engage with life, especially in unjust situations, just as Jesus would encourage the raising of women's voices and allow for the full development of who they are."[2] Further, "The African Synod's desire for the church to be salt of the earth and light of the world calls for efforts toward reconciliation, justice, and peace. In this task African women can play an irreplaceable role."[3] Yet most official church texts conceal the realities of African women's lives, the oppressions they endure, and the struggles they face. Along with culturally generated biases and prejudices, these omissions contradict official rhetoric that celebrates the complementary roles, qualities, and contributions of women.

Nigerian theologian Teresa Okure has remarked that the marginalization of women "distorts the image of God in woman, denies woman her baptismal right and status in Christ, and greatly impoverishes not only the woman but the entire human community by belittling, killing and suppressing the God-given talents of women."[4] Her view constitutes a telling critique of Christianity.

Christianity came to Africa wearing a distinctly Western garb. The expression of the Christian God was foreign to the African worldview, even though Christianity is a religion that has traveled widely and has been adopted into many cultures. Christianity needs to be transformed again and again in our own day to include the worldviews of those outside the West and those of women, especially in African church and society.

Jesus is now very present in Africa, and he is being named and recognized as African. The church in Africa is growing and demanding its own identity in the Christian world. There is a strong and definitive movement toward an African Jesus. Women are not absent from this movement—see, for example, Diane Stinton's groundbreaking work on African Christology.[5] However, an important question emerges: Who is Christ for African women?

Ghanaian theologian Mercy Amba Oduyoye argues that many of our churches in Africa have—perhaps unwittingly—contributed to the loss of African women's identities through the absorption of Western culture.[6] African women's relationship with their culture—their families, cultural rituals and songs, dances and stories, proverbs, clothing, and last but not least, their religious beliefs and practices, are a buried treasure waiting to be discovered by the African Church.

In Chinua Achebe's *Things Fall Apart*, the heroic figure, Okonkwo, having been exiled from his fatherland, moves his entire family to his motherland. His maternal uncle's welcome reads as a poignant testimony to the untapped potential of the African woman that lies buried under the detritus of patriarchy and misogyny:

> Why is Okonkwo with us today? This is not his clan. We are only his mother's kinsmen. He does not belong here. He is an exile, condemned for seven years to live in a strange land....It's true that a child belongs to its father. But when a father beats his child, it seeks sympathy in its mother's hut. A man belongs to his fatherland when things are good and

life is sweet. But when there is sorrow and bitterness
he finds refuge in his motherland. Your mother is
there to protect you. [7]

The first identity of an African woman is seen as mother
and wife, and the roles of motherhood and womanhood are
intertwined. However, the church's rush to endorse woman's
role as procreator and helpmate often bypasses the positive val-
orization of the *personhood* of the African woman *in herself.*

Identifying women as mothers with a biological function
to reproduce is a societal construction of gender that dehu-
manizes women. African women have been socialized into
thinking of themselves as worthless if they cannot bear children, yet all African women should see themselves as mothers
of life—as intelligent educators and mentors, appreciating and
affirming the beauty and gift of African womanhood.

With the advent of globalization and technology, African
women are reflecting more and more on their experiences in
the light of the gospel, in the light of the Qu'ran, and in the
light of African Indigenous Religion. They are beginning to ask
pertinent questions that relate to freedom, dignity, respect, and
equality for all humans. As Pope Francis reminds us in *Evangelii
Gaudium*, "The People of God is incarnate in the peoples of the
earth, each of which has its own culture....Understood in this
way, culture embraces the totality of a people's life" (*EG* 115).

A Kenyan proverb says, "Nobody can use another person's
teeth to smile."[8] To reflect theologically on African women's lives
entails listening and paying attention, while resisting the lure of
facile judgments. As Nigerian theologian Agbonkhianmeghe
Orobator asserts, "Doing theology is not an exercise in conceptual weightlessness. It develops within the particular culture and
context of the community that attempts to utter a word or two on
the reality of God and the demands of faith for daily living. This
word does not defy the law of gravity."[9]

To bridge the gap between official Church pronounce-
ments and African women's lives and cultures, we need to
unmask the contradictions and generate new paradigms and

narratives capable of sustaining the hopes and responding to the aspirations of African women for full inclusion in the community called church in Africa and the world.

NOTES

1. Pope John Paul II, "Post-Synodal Apostolic Exhortation" (*Ecclesia in Africa*), 1995, http://w2.vatican.va/content/john-paul-ii/en/apost_exhortations/documents/hf_jp-ii_exh_14091995_ecclesia-in-africa.html; Synod of Bishops, "Propositions of the Second Special Assembly for Africa", 2009, http://www.vatican.va/roman_curia/synod/documents/rc_synod_doc_20091023_elenco-prop-finali_en.html.

2. Anne Arabome, "'Woman You Are Set Free!' Women and Discipleship in the Church," in *Reconciliation, Justice, and Peace: The Second African Synod*, ed. Agbonkhianmeghe E. Orobator (Maryknoll NY: Orbis Books, 2011), 122.

3. Ibid., 124.

4. "Synod for Africa Opens to High Hopes, but Realism," *The National Catholic Reporter*, October 2, 2009, http://ncronline.org/print/15163.

5. Diane B. Stinton, *Jesus of Africa: Voices of Contemporary African Christology* (Maryknoll NY: Orbis Books, 2004), 5–6.

6. Mercy Amba Oduyoye, "Acting as Women," in *African Theology Today*, ed. Emmanuel Katongole (Scranton: The University of Scranton Press, 2002), 179.

7. Chinua Achebe, *Things Fall Apart* (New York: Anchor Books, 1994), 133–35.

8. Julia Stewart, *African Proverbs and Wisdom: A Collection for Every Day of the Year from More Than Forty African Nations* (New York: Kensington Publishing Corp, 1997), 128.

9. Agbonkhianmeghe E. Orobator, *Theology Brewed in an African Pot* (Maryknoll, NY: Orbis Books, 2008), 152.

LATIN AMERICAN WOMEN

In Mary's Footsteps or in Her Shadow?

CAROLINA DEL RÍO MENA
(TRANS. RHONDA MISKA MA)

Inside my head I heard my grandmother's words: "Only boys catch tadpoles." Only boys. I hesitated, but Sweet nudged me with the jar. Soon I was elbow-deep in the brown water, chasing after the rich, darting life before me. I was reveling in a new universe, and it was one of the grander times of my girlhood. It was the day I learned to challenge the tight, tidy categories of what was expected and possible in my world. Like the tadpoles, I was molting into a new being.[1]

Sue Monk Kidd's story describes two paradigmatic situations: first, that there are activities reserved for men which we women internalize very early; second, as women we must dare to catch tadpoles and enter into that masculine world of norms, not simply for the sake of the challenge but rather as a way—perhaps the only way—of attaining full humanization.

The institution of the Church, its spheres of power and decision making, and the relationship between men and women in

This is an edited version of an unpublished paper given at a symposium on "Women in the Church: Perspectives in Dialogue" at the Pontifical University Antonianum, Rome on April 28, 2015. The full Spanish version is available on the website (www.catholicwomenspeak.com).

Latin America, are today that muddy water that offers opportunities for tadpole catching and renewing the culture to make it more inclusive and equal. Our evangelizing challenge is to bring into practice and accompany the cultural changes taking place. As a framework for this essay, I want to offer some material from this continent of hope, as it was once called by John Paul II.

A 2014 study reports that Latin American people are living "according to some beliefs which are stronger than the impact of development, more resistant to change than expected."[2] Only in Uruguay and Chile is agnosticism/atheism gaining ground as evidence of secularization.[3] Yet the 2010 Report of the United Nations Development Program (UNDP) on Gender Equality concludes that "traditionalism and *machismo* still exercise an important influence in Chilean society."[4] In other words, accelerated secularization has not brought about a corresponding transformation in men's roles. Men's reluctance to modify their behavior and to assume responsibilities in the household to permit greater female autonomy limits the development of women's capacities.

In this context, I believe that our Church has a great responsibility for the promotion of change. Pope Francis has said that "all institutions, including the ecclesial community, are called to guarantee the freedom of choice of women, so that they may have the opportunity to assume social and ecclesial responsibilities, in a manner in harmony with family life."[5] To leave behind the vision of women exclusively as their auxiliary function of producing offspring fills us with hope but, even though things have changed, there is still a long road before us in Latin America, as the Latin American pope knows.

Two unique phenomena are vitally important for the identity of our continent: machismo and what is called *marianismo*. Machismo is discrimination based on the belief that men are superior to women and, as the 2010 UNPD study shows, it remains deeply rooted in our societies.

I will spend more time on *marianismo* because our continent is a Marian continent, and the symbolic significance of Mary is complex and ambiguous. For some women the suffering mother who understands and embraces them is a source of consolation. For others, her supposed or apparent passivity are unacceptable and they cannot identify with her. For many women, Mary has modeled their womanhood; for others, she has been the explosive source of deep rebellion and internal ruptures.

This Marian cult is the product of a complex process of religious syncretism beginning with the Spanish conquest in the sixteenth century. In particular, the appearance of the Virgin of Guadalupe to the indigenous Juan Diego has played a vital role because, in the words of anthropologist Sonia Montecino, "it wrote a history which remains as a shared footprint in the substratum of our mestiza culture."[6] The Virgin of Guadalupe has transcended borders, installing herself as the patroness of the Latin American continent. Her relationship with Juan Diego has influenced the relationship between men and women in the whole continent. Guadalupe has constituted the "configuration of being man and being woman under symbolic categories of being son and being mother, respectively."[7]

What emerges as symbol is not Mary the woman of Nazareth, but the one-dimensionality of her maternity that finds fertile ground on a fatherless mestizo continent. Imagination and popular religiosity tend to compare Mary with "the single mother," evoking "our foundational history: present mestizo or Indian mother and absent Spanish father."[8] The overrepresentation of Mary's maternal features are constitutive of the exaltation of the Virgin Mother that extends across our continent. It is for this reason that, when Latin American women do theology, we discover the "triggering function and critique which contains our own religious experience as women which makes necessary a revision of the Marian model...to recover [in Mary] the current and prophetic paradigm of a reconciled and actualized humanity."[9] We women who do theology are mobilizing ourselves to recover a more whole image of Mary as poor believing woman of Nazareth.

I have no doubt about the importance of Mary's maternity in salvation history: it was she who educated Jesus, who taught him to eat, to talk, to pray. She taught him the equal dignity and worth of men and women that, later, Jesus lived. However, the unmeasured exaltation of Mary's maternity has left in shadow the most relevant part of her experience as a believing Jewish woman: her capacity to receive the Word creatively and transform life. Therefore, removing the focus of Mary's maternal role and focusing on other emerging roles such as friend, disciple, sister, and prophet of God will permit us to see again and draw close to Mary in our communities.

The search for a more just order and God's truth is not work that can be given up. Glimpsing and intuiting the mystery of God should move us to practice new ways of relating and new perspectives about humanity. It is necessary to submerge ourselves in that muddy water to search for tadpoles because the equality of men and women, respecting their differences, both created in the image of God, is a gospel mandate that must be made true in history—in personal history, in structural history, and in political and ecclesial history.

NOTES

1. Sue Monk Kidd, *When the Heart Waits: Spiritual Direction for Life's Sacred Questions* (New York: HarperCollins, 1992), 18.

2. Corporación Latinobarómetro, *Las religiones en tiempos del Papa Francisco*, April 16, 2014, http://www.latinobarometro.org/latNewsShowMore.jsp?evYEAR=2014&evMONTH=4.

3. In the Latinobarómetro report, secularization is a reference only to the increase of people who declare themselves "agnostic/atheist" or "without religion." A more in-depth study on the process of secularization and secularity is found in Ana Maria Stuven Vattier, *Secularización y laicidad en Chile: una interpretación del debate sobre tolerancia* (Santiago: Universidad Católica de Chile, 2012); Roberto Blancarte, "Dilemas del pasado y retos del presente para la laicidad en América Latina," in *La religión en la esfera pública chilena: laicidad o secularización?*, ed. Ana Maria Stuven (Santiago: Universidad Diego Portales, 2013), 95–130.

4. United Nations Development Program, Human Development Report 2010—Chile, http://hdr.undp.org/en/search-reports?country=CL&type=All&field_year_tid=124&field_theme_tid=All&field_translation_tid=All.

5. Pope Francis, "Address to Participants in the Plenary Assembly of the Pontifical Council for Culture," February 7, 2015, https://w2.vatican.va/content/francesco/en/speeches/2015/february/documents/papa-francesco_20150207_pontificio-consiglio-cultura.html.

6. Sonia Montecino, *Madres y huachos. Alegorías del mestizaje chileno* (Santiago: Ed. Catalonia, 2007), 71.

7. Ibid.

8. Ibid., 85.

9. Azcuy Virginia, "Reencontrar a María como modelo. Interpelación feminista a la mariología actual," *Proyecto 39* (2001): 163–85, at 166.

THE MOTHERHOOD OF THE CHURCH

Mary, the Quotidian, and the People of God

CRISTINA LLEDO GOMEZ

The short title of my PhD thesis was "The Church as Mother." Those who hear this often respond, "Oh, you're doing a thesis on Mary." This is a natural connection as Mary, the *theotokos*, is the "Mother of God." At Vatican II, she was additionally named "Mother of the Church" and its *ecclesiatype* (*LG* 63). However, to me this response was frustrating since the motherhood of the Church both antedates and transcends its modeling through Mary's maternity. We need only look to the use of *Mater Ecclesia* by early patristic writers such as Irenaeus, Tertullian, and Cyprian, but also at the early baptismal fonts of the second through to the fifth centuries, to realize this.[1]

Devotion to Mary has played a significant role in the development of my personal faith and I recognize its place in the Church. However, while Mary is an *ecclesiatype*, the image of "mother" has both universal and cultural connotations, derived from the lived experience of women, which must be recognized if the metaphor or image of "Mother Church" is to be employed in a meaningful way.

Mary's maternity has been associated with perfect mothering in a way that does not reflect the quotidian experiences of mothers. Except in a few scriptural instances (such as Jesus lost in the temple [Luke 2:41–52] and Mary at the foot of the cross

[John 19:25]), her elevated maternity represents an unbalanced view of motherhood, reflecting only the positives of "blissful gratification and tenderness" but negating the "exquisite suffering…of bitter resentment and raw-edged nerves."[2] Even at the foot of the cross, Mary's suffering is often idealized, representing an elevated moment of serene and dignified grief rather than the universal experience of mothers suffering in the quotidian.

Connected to this maternal suffering is the burden of living up to the image of the "Good Mother." Sarah Ruddick explains,

> An idealized figure of the Good Mother casts a long shadow on many actual mothers' lives. Our days include few if any perfect moments, perfect children perfectly cared for.…Many mothers who live in the Good Mother's shadow, knowing that they have been angry and resentful and remembering episodes of violence and neglect, come to feel that their lives are riddled with shameful secrets that even the closest friends can't share.[3]

Is there room for the image of Mother Church to reflect such realities, where mothering is not only toward infants but also toward toddlers, adolescents, teenagers, and even adult children? Can this image embrace the exchange between mother and child as they both give and receive and are challenged by one another? Can the Mother Church image incorporate the fact that children themselves grow and become mothers to others?

Too often at Vatican II, particularly in *Lumen Gentium*, members of the Church were called "children" and encouraged to place themselves under the maternal care of Mary. In this, the members of the Church are infantilized rather than encouraged to grow in faith and become spiritual mothers themselves. This overshadows the call to all the baptized to engage in the mission of the Church and therefore share in her motherhood, as *Lumen Gentium* states:

> The Virgin in her own life lived an example of that maternal love, by which it behooves that all should be animated who cooperate in the apostolic mission of the Church for the regeneration of people. (*LG* 65)

This passage recognizes that all Christians are called to be spiritual mothers—to give birth to Christ in their hearts and to participate in the apostolic mission of the Church motivated by a maternal love of humankind. St. Augustine too describes his community as containing both spiritual infants and mothers. In the following passage he challenges all to mature to that motherhood of the Church reflected in Mary:

> Just as Mary gave birth in her womb as a virgin to Christ, so let the members of Christ give birth in their minds, and in this way you will be the mothers of Christ. It isn't something out of your reach, not something beyond your powers, not something incompatible with what you are. You became children, become mothers too.[4]

The image of the Church as Mother and her members as her eternally infant children may be the very image that obstructs the full, conscious, and active participation of the entire people of God (*SC* 14). The maternal ecclesial image may even need to be extended to include the real-life dynamic of the child growing and undergoing a necessary stage of separation from the mother in order that the Church member may grow in adult faith and become a self-responsible, accountable, and mature adult in the Church. To move past the "Good Mother" or idealized Marian imagery and draw upon the reality of contemporary motherhood would provide a different web of associations about Mother Church, which in our complex and diverse context could breathe new life into the maternal ecclesial image.

Pope Francis, whose favorite ecclesial image is Mother Church,[5] images her as the people of God engaged in its mission. He said at a general audience in 2014,

All who are baptized, men and women, together we are the Church. So often in our lives we do not bear witness of this motherhood of the Church, of this maternal courage of the Church! So often we are cowards! Let us then entrust ourselves to Mary, that She as mother of our firstborn brother, Jesus, may teach us to have the same maternal spirit toward our brothers and sisters, with the sincere capacity to welcome, to forgive, to give strength and to instil trust and hope. This is what a mother does.[6]

Like St. Augustine, Pope Francis calls the people of God to grow up and reflect the motherhood of the Church—in other words, to become mothers to others themselves. Such an approach, along with a renewed appreciation of the multifaceted realities of motherhood, show the potential of moving the traditional metaphor of "Holy Mother Church" beyond a well-worn cliché that is almost synonymous with the magisterium, toward a rich and meaningful image with a powerful network of associations that can be transformative of the Church's self-understanding.

NOTES

1. Cf. Joseph Conrad Plumpe, *Mater Ecclesia: An Inquiry into the Concept of the Church as Mother in Early Christianity* (Washington, DC: The Catholic University of America Press, 1943); Robin M. Jensen, "Mater Ecclesia and Fons Aeterna: The Church and Her Womb in Ancient Christian Tradition," in *A Feminist Companion to Patristic Literature*, ed. Amy-Jill Levine with Maria Mayo Robbins (New York: T&T Clark International, 2008).

2. Adrienne Rich, "Anger and Tenderness" from *Of "Woman" Born: Motherhood as Experience and Institution*, in *Mother Reader: Essential Writings on Motherhood*, ed. Moyra Davey (New York: Seven Stories Press, 2001), 81.

3. Sara Ruddick, *Maternal Thinking: Toward a Politics of Peace* (Boston: Beacon Press, 1989), 31.

4. Augustine, "Sermon 72A," ch. 8, in *The Works of St. Augustine: A Translation for the 21st Century*, trans. Edmund Hill, ed. John Rotelle (New York: New City Press, 1991).

5. Cf. Pope Francis, General Weekly Audience, St. Peter's Square, Wednesday, September 18, 2013, https://w2.vatican.va/content/francesco/en/audiences/2013/documents/papa-francesco_20130918_udienza-generale.html.

6. Pope Francis, General Weekly Audience, St. Peter's Square, Wednesday, September 3, 2014, https://w2.vatican.va/content/francesco/en/audiences/2014/documents/papa-francesco_20140903_udienza-generale.html.

TRADITIONS AND TRANSFORMATIONS

Catholic and Muslim Women in Dialogue

TRISH MADIGAN

In the 2000s, I belonged to a group of Muslim and Catholic women who were meeting together over morning tea, getting to know each other and building relationships between our women's communities. We met monthly for ten years. I came to understand how Muslim women experience the many beautiful gifts received from their tradition while, at the same time, they recognize the constraints that their tradition places on them. The same thing happened for Catholic women who were able to articulate the beauty of their tradition, while also acknowledging the blocks they experienced.

Both Catholic and Muslim women came to acknowledge a kind of fundamentalism about the place of women in their religious traditions, and we shared that experience. Some typical comments were the following:

Muslim woman: The misinterpretation of verses or injunctions in the Qur'an and the misapplication of *shari'a* law affect women. We have scholars who give correct interpretations but there are others who don't have enough knowledge of the Arabic language, who follow a narrow interpretation. It is an abuse of *shari'a* not to relate the injunction to the circumstances of the revelation.

Catholic woman: There is a commonality of the exclusion of women, whatever the tradition. I think it is experienced differently but when you analyze it you can still see it. It's a kind of exclusion by the patriarchal system that always excludes and then goes and puts energy into protecting itself. The system protects itself by theologizing about the exclusion. I think that sums it up.

Through their dialogue the women realized that alternative models, inclusive of women, were possible and that their respective religious traditions contained the spiritual, historical, and theological resources needed to reshape and renew these traditions. The Muslim women stressed that the real purpose of *shari'a* law is to protect individuals from injustice and to make life "easy and fair and just," while the Catholic women experienced their belief in the resurrection of Jesus as a source of hope and empowerment. All the women were acting, at least implicitly, in their belief that the full flourishing of all humanity is dependent on improving the status of women.

In fact, we agreed that there is a universal challenge that all women of faith come face-to-face with in their religious traditions. As women, we find that our religious traditions have been defining us over the centuries, but it has been men defining women. Certain groups of men have defined what women's role is in society, what their nature is, and what their contribution is—usually as mothers. There has been a failure to recognize that women's lives are multidimensional and that women have enormously varied ways of contributing to society. As one woman commented,

> It's interesting that women are being defined, but the religions don't sit around defining men and their role—that's just seen as taken for granted, and women's role has somehow got to be discussed and defined.

The challenge all women face in our respective religions is to be included as part of the mainstream. We want to have our gifts recognized; we want to be able to contribute to the whole of the religion, not just the one small section that is pigeon-holed as "women's role." We are people with a whole range of skills, and we want to be able to develop fully as human beings and contribute all our skills. That's what women are striving for.

I think this is what's happening in the Catholic Church at the moment. Women are seeing that our gifts are needed at all levels of the Church—not only at the parish level or in secondary roles. Women have gifts in leadership that are not being used by the Church, and both the Church and women themselves are suffering diminishment as a consequence.

When you move out to the secular world, you find there are Muslim women leaders in government offices, there are Catholic women leaders in government offices—in Australia, we have had a woman prime minister and women as state premiers at the same time. So we have seen women in leadership and now people everywhere are saying, "Why can't we have this kind of leadership in the religious world as well?"

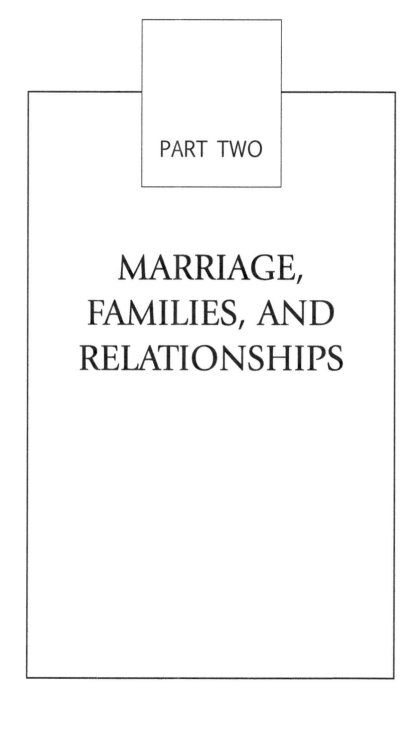

PART TWO

MARRIAGE, FAMILIES, AND RELATIONSHIPS

INTRODUCTION
TO PART TWO

The transformations taking place in women's roles and identities have had a profound influence on our most intimate relationships. In 2014, in the light of rapidly changing values and expectations, the Catholic bishops embarked on a far-reaching process of reflection on the family. Although the discussions of the bishops were wide-ranging and often bold in the questions they addressed, the wisdom of women was almost entirely lacking from these deliberations.

Women are the custodians of family life and human relationships. In every culture, they remain the primary care givers for the young, the elderly, and the vulnerable. Young girls are conditioned to accept these roles and to subsume their own desires for personal development and self-fulfilment to dedicate themselves to serving others. While such service is fundamental to the Christian understanding of neighborly love, women today are realizing that love of others does not require the negation of self. Jesus commands us to love our neighbors as ourselves. Discussing this commandment, St. Thomas Aquinas reminds us that we ourselves belong among the good things of God that are to be loved, and we should desire for ourselves what we desire for others (ST II-II, 25, 4). Women today are asking how they might realize their human dignity and equality in the context of loving and responsible domestic and social relationships in which all are able to flourish.

Such visions of flourishing are fragile and sometimes even seem futile, for we live in a wounded world of broken relationships and failed attempts to realize our dreams of wholeness. Ours is a faith that calls not for perfection but for forgiveness, healing, and redemption in Christ. Many of the essays in this section grapple with painful and complex realities, as women of faith bring theological and personal reflection to bear on the dilemmas and challenges of modern relationships and family life.

Julie Clague offers an overview of surveys that confirm that there is "a significant disjunction" between the Church's official teaching on marriage and family, and the diverse values and practices by way of which Catholics express the being of the Church in different social and cultural contexts. Clague also points out that there is broad consensus among Catholics with regard to many of the challenges facing families because of social and economic pressures, violence and conflict, diseases, loneliness, and bereavement. She concludes that only through greater participation of the lay faithful in the institutional Church will it be possible "to close the gap between theological rhetoric and pastoral realities."

Lisa Sowle Cahill considers theological approaches to the relationship between family life, marriage, and sexual relationships. She argues that "a contemporary ethics of family should be concerned with the justice and the supportive nature of intergenerational relationships, not primarily with approved or disapproved sex." This shift in emphasis calls for an embrace of Pope Francis's vision of a Church in which gospel values of forgiveness, hope, and resurrection create a space for mercy and "neighborly empathy" rather than "righteous judgment" with regard to the struggles and sorrows of family life.

Clare Watkins offers a nuanced reflection upon the ways in which such struggles constitute the holiness of ordinary families, not in spite of but often because of their transgressions and failures. In an essay that resonates with Gomez's essay in part 1, Watkins argues that it is "a failure of its maternal wisdom" when Mother Church regards teaching as "the handing down of rules" rather than a process of unconditional loving and growing through the different ages and stages of human development. It is in and through the transgressive challenges of family life that "a profundity of compassion, grace, and peace" can be experienced.

Sara Maitland offers a robust and incisive challenge to the idea of "complementarity," pointing out that appeals to "natural" complementarity have served to justify the oppression of women in ways that invite comparison with "the rhetoric of apartheid." She argues that, in a world in which women still suffer the effects of inequality and violence across cultures and contexts, the "philosophical problem about gender and its meanings" is also a question of justice. What is needed is a shared endeavor to better understand and describe differences between individuals, and an acknowledgement that "sometimes we get things wrong."

Tina Beattie revisits the medieval cult of St. Anne, and asks what it might teach us today about different ways of representing holy families. She refers to late medieval iconography that depicts the conception of the Virgin as a tender embrace between her elderly parents, Joachim and Anne. She also considers representations of St. Anne and the Virgin in various contexts that affirm the mother-daughter relationship and show the infant Christ being cared for in maternal kinship groupings. Reflecting on grandmothers caring for HIV/AIDS orphans in sub-Saharan Africa and on changing models of family life, Beattie suggests that the cult of St. Anne might offer alternative ways of envisioning what it means to be a family, beyond the model of the nuclear family that emerged in the context of the modern state.

Margaret Watson describes the dilemmas she faces as a recent convert to Catholicism, because her Baptist husband of forty years cannot take communion with her when they attend Mass together. A particular problem is the inconsistency of different priests with regard to whether or not non-Catholic Christians can receive communion. Some say, "We must keep the rules of the Church," to which her response is, "What about the urging of the Holy Spirit?"

The next three essays by Alison Concannon Kennedy, Pippa Bonner, and Anna Cannon offer personal accounts of divorce and remarriage. As the Church seeks a pastoral solution to the challenge of divorced and remarried Catholics, these women speak of the grief of eucharistic separation, which so often exacerbates the anguish of divorce and the fragile process of learning to love again. They show a concern for the care of children and the nurturing of faith through and beyond marital breakdown, offering insights into the trauma of divorce and possible pastoral processes that can support the transition to healing and new life.

Contraception remains one of the most vexed questions with regard to Church teaching on marriage, being the area where Catholic practice is most clearly out of line with magisterial teaching. Jean Porter's essay examines the status of that teaching in the light of the Catholic theological tradition's consistent affirmation of the value of procreation. She suggests that the current teaching on contraception might come to be quietly dropped, using the example of the marriage debt—the teaching that spouses who deny their partners sex on request are guilty of serious sin—as an example of a previous teaching to which this has already happened. In the case of contraception this process would recognize that, while the Church safeguards revelation, it does so in the context of human limitations—a point that, she suggests, invites further reflection.

The next three essays once again move us from theological analysis to personal reflection with regard to contraception and the Church's promotion of Natural Family Planning (NFP). Rachel Espinoza and Tawny Horner, both practitioners of NFP, give a searingly honest account of the tensions this method can create in a marriage. Olive Barnes, Amelia Beck, and Giovanna Solari-Masson explain why they decided to use alternative forms of birth control because of damaging experiences of the failure of NFP in the lives of either their mothers or themselves. Emma Jane Harris writes as a "millennial," a young woman who represents a new generation of Catholics who follow their own consciences around issues of sexuality and contraception. She writes, "While the Church works out its complex and contradictory relationship with gender, sexuality, and the millennial generation, I have a life to live and work to do."

Another challenge facing the Church today is that of same-sex relationships. Margaret Farley offers a theological analysis of arguments that might support same-sex marriage, in the light of new insights about human sexuality and changing social and economic circumstances. Mutually pledged commitment is now seen to be at the heart of marriage—"a permanent blending of loves" in which a commitment to fruitfulness "can take many forms." If this is so, Farley asks, why should same-sex marriages not also be "experiences of the presence of God—manifest not only to the partners in marriage but to the Church and the world"?

We turn to the voices of personal experience to illuminate these theological reflections. Sophie Stanes and Deborah Woodman movingly describe their experience of civil partnership as Catholic women with a deep commitment to one another and their church community. Having lost their premature twin babies, conceived through IVF, they are able to say that they have "seen the Church at its best and its worst." They have experienced warm support and prayer from their community and from some priests, and have been harshly rejected by others—an experience that "leaves us as second-class citizens who give all we can but risk everything when we ask." Like Margaret Watson's experience of her husband's exclusion from the Eucharist, their reality is of a vexing inconsistency in the ways in which individual priests apply church teaching in their pastoral practice.

Ursula Halligan describes her tormenting experience of realizing as an Irish Catholic teenager that she was gay. She lived much of her adult life in secret self-loathing and loneliness. The Irish referendum on same-sex marriage emboldened her to speak out publicly about being gay, in the hopes that, "if my story helps even one seventeen-year-old schoolgirl, struggling with her sexuality, it will have been worth it."

Eve Tushnet discusses her decision to adopt a celibate lifestyle as a gay woman after her conversion to Catholicism. In a nuanced and pragmatic reflection, she explains her reasons for embracing the Catholic faith, and her willingness to accept teachings that she might not fully understand. She suggests that gay Catholics, "by leading lives of fruitful, creative love,…can offer proof that sexual restraint isn't a death sentence (or an especially boring form of masochism). Celibacy can offer some of us radical freedom to serve others."

In a theological reflection on Thomist virtue theory, Katie Grimes questions the argument put forward by Tushnet and other celibate gay Catholics that acceptance of their homosexual identity is consistent with respecting church teaching that homosexual acts are "intrinsically disordered." Not so, suggests Grimes, for while "the magisterium tells homosexual persons they can be but they must not do," this directive is not consistent with the way in which virtue ethics understands the relationship between desiring and acting. "If one should not do, then neither should one be," argues Grimes, adding that "perhaps lesbian and gay Catholics struggle to find a home within ordinary Catholic parishes because there is no place for them in the pages of magisterial teaching."

Finally in this extensive exploration of Catholic women's relationships and sexual identities, we hear from a religious sister about the positive benefits of female celibacy, and from a single woman who has learned to live creatively on the periphery of society. Janette Gray refers to the lack of attention paid to women's celibacy in the context of religious vows, an oversight resulting from the preoccupation with problems associated with male celibacy. She draws on her research into women's experiences of celibacy to argue that "abstinence from sexual activity can be understood not to devalue sex, the body, or women's sexuality, but to represent wider human experiences of sexuality and relationships than sexual intercourse." An incarnational celibacy that is open to sexuality "reveals that God is found in the diversity of creation and human encounters, not in narcissism nor exclusively in the isolation of the couple."

Patricia Stoat describes how she learned to embrace a life of solitude and to celebrate it as "a vocation, an art form, a lifestyle, a way," even when this might not have been the life she would have chosen. Drawing on biblical and historical examples, she suggests that single women belong among those who are on the margins where "the creative heart" is to be found, for in the "the new reality" that reflects the Church, "the outsider is the insider."

These theological essays and personal reflections constitute "a narrative enchiridion," to use Cardinal Ravasi's expression quoted earlier. They offer some insight into the expansive range of Catholic women's ideas and experiences with regard to pastoral questions facing the Church today. It is the longest and most substantial section in the book, because it addresses some of the demanding issues facing women as they seek to express their faith in Christ amidst the complex realities of their daily lives. As we said in the introduction, these accounts are not intended to be read instead of but rather alongside the witness given by married couples who addressed the Synod on the Family in 2014. When the perspectives offered here are included, a more rounded picture of Catholic family life emerges than the one that is formed when only officially sanctioned voices are permitted to speak. Even so, this remains a partial snapshot, for many voices are still to be heard from within the abundant diversity of the global Church.

CATHOLICS, FAMILIES, AND THE SYNOD OF BISHOPS

Views from the Pews

JULIE CLAGUE

On October 8, 2013, Pope Francis convoked the Third Extraordinary General Assembly of the Synod of Bishops, for October 5–19, 2014, on the theme "Pastoral challenges of the family in the context of evangelisation." This assembly would precede the Ordinary General Assembly of the Synod of Bishops scheduled for October 4–25, 2015 on the theme "Jesus Christ reveals the mystery and vocation of the family," thereby creating an unprecedented two-stage process of reflection on the family by the synod of Bishops.

After detailing some of the specific issues that have become "a pastoral challenge in the Church's evangelizing mission concerning the family," the Preparatory Document (*PD*) emphasizes that "reflection on these issues by the Synod of Bishops" is "much needed and urgent," and that "vast expectations exist concerning the decisions which are to be made pastorally regarding the family" (*PD* 1).

Half of the document is taken up with a series of thirty-nine questions directed to the particular Churches across the globe. Archbishop (now Cardinal) Baldisseri, secretary general

This is an edited extract from an essay that was first published as Julie Clague, "Catholics, Families and the Synod of Bishops: Views from the Pews," special issue: Faith, Family and Fertility, *The Heythrop Journal*, 55, no. 6 (November 2014): 985–1008. Published with permission.

of the synod of Bishops, requested that the Preparatory Document be distributed to every level of the Church, including the grassroots, in order to generate the maximum feedback and to gather evidence and insights concerning the topics covered in the preparatory questions.

The synod working document, the *Instrumentum laboris* (*IL*), published in June 2014, confirms that many (probably in the region of several hundred thousand) Catholic individuals and groups participated in the consultation process. Most of these responses and observations are not in the public domain. However, the Austrian, Flemish and French-speaking Belgian, German, Japanese, Maltese, and Swiss Episcopal Conferences made public their submissions.[1]

In broad terms, the findings confirm a significant disjunction between the vision of marriage and family promoted by the Church in its official teaching and the various attitudes, values, lifestyles, and practices that can be witnessed in the diverse social and cultural contexts in which the Church has its being: "A vast majority of responses highlight the growing conflict between the values on marriage and the family as proposed by the Church and the globally diversified social and cultural situations" (*IL* 15). Aspects of teaching that tend to be "overlooked" include those involving "birth control, divorce and remarriage, homosexuality, cohabitation, fidelity, premarital sex, *in vitro* fertilization" (*IL* 13). The working document speaks of the "demise of the concept of the natural law" (*IL* 26), one of the crown jewels of the Catholic intellectual tradition, and the theological and ethical underpinning upon which much of Catholic teaching on sexual morality relies.

In February 2014, a Spanish-language media company, Univision Communications, published the results of a global survey of Catholic opinion—one of several surveys undertaken in relation to the synodal process. The survey was based on data gathered from 12,038 self-identified adult Catholics in twelve countries. The countries selected were those with the eleven highest populations of Catholics: Brazil; Mexico; Philippines; United States of America; Italy; Colombia; France; Poland;

Spain; Democratic Republic of Congo; Argentina; and a twelfth country, Uganda (in order to allow for a better representation of sub-Saharan Africa).[2] Together, these nations account for 60 percent of the world's Catholic population.[3]

The findings indicate wide disparities between the views of ordinary Catholics on the issues surveyed and Church teachings on these issues:

> Taken together, these findings suggest an extraordinary disconnect between the church's basic teachings on the fundamental issues of family and pastoral responsibilities and the viewpoints currently held by many of the world's more than 1 billion Catholics.[4]

A majority of Catholics expressed views on contraception, on abortion, and on the admission of the divorced and remarried to the sacraments at odds with the teaching of the Church. Two-thirds of Catholics oppose marriage between two persons of the same sex. Half of those surveyed believe priests should be allowed to marry,[5] and 45 percent favor the admission of women to the ministerial priesthood.[6] The Univision survey is not without its limitations, but as a large-scale representative survey of six in ten of the world's Catholic population, it makes an important contribution to our knowledge of Catholic opinion around the world.

Work remains to be done in articulating how, precisely, sociological research informs the tasks of theology, and how theological ideas such as doctrinal reception and the *sensus fidei* might relate to observable social phenomena within the Church while, all the time, avoiding the error of reading sociology as theology. Many of the questions raised by these issues are addressed in the International Theological Commission's "*Sensus Fidei* in the Life of the Church" (*SF*),[7] which also highlights the contribution made by the laity "with regard to the development of the moral teaching of the Church" and "in discerning the Christian understanding of appropriate human behaviour in accordance with the Gospel" (*SF* 73). Surely, the

Church should recognize its particular dependency upon the experience and expertise of laypeople in discerning its response to the pastoral challenges facing families? On the question of the nonreception of Church teaching, the document states,

> Problems arise when the majority of the faithful remain indifferent to doctrinal or moral decisions taken by the magisterium or when they positively reject them. This lack of reception may indicate a weakness or a lack of faith on the part of the people of God, caused by an insufficiently critical embrace of contemporary culture. But in some cases it may indicate that certain decisions have been taken by those in authority without due consideration of the experience and the *sensus fidei* of the faithful, or without sufficient consultation of the faithful by the magisterium (*SF* 123).

Recent research means that there is now a large body of survey and other evidence available to the bishops. The picture of Catholicism we receive from this research is complex and varied, as one might expect for a Church of over one billion members. A substantial disconnect is evident, however, throughout many parts of the globe between Church teaching and Catholic attitudes on some issues of family life.

Prior to the synod assemblies, Pope Francis ensured there was a consultation of the faithful of unprecedented scale. The consultation uncovered the extent of suffering experienced by Catholics:

> Many of the difficulties highlighted in the responses and observations reveal the agonizing situation of people today when faced with the subjects of love, the generation of life, the reciprocity between man and woman and fatherhood and motherhood (*IL* 122).

It also confirmed that, on certain questions, the Church's magisterium and large numbers of the faithful appear to inhabit different Catholic worlds. The nonreception of Church teaching represents a crisis for Catholicism that requires action. Nonetheless, this should not be allowed to overshadow the broad consensus that exists across the Church with regard to a large number of critical challenges facing families today that were identified during the consultation process. These include the following: domestic abuse and violence; incest; human trafficking; sex tourism; substance abuse; prostitution; pornography; addictions to gambling, gaming, and Internet use; the harmful effects of information and communications technology on relationships; the impact of work, unemployment, and job insecurity on family life; the impact of migration; the excessive educational expectations laid on children; conflicts and war; the plight of displaced peoples; the impact of AIDS and other diseases; loneliness and bereavement (see *IL* 66–79). If there are some pastoral challenges to marriage and family life where the *consensus fidelium* appears to be lacking, on many urgent issues it is very much in evidence. Catholics are united with others across the globe, at the grassroots and at high level governance, in promoting compassion and justice for families and family members.

Synod assemblies cannot do all the work of discernment required of the people of God. New institutional mechanisms must be found to allow the lay faithful to play their full part in the joint task of discerning the *sensus fidei* of the faithful, and in helping to close the gap between theological rhetoric and pastoral realities.

NOTES

1. Links to the synod responses that are in the public domain can be found on the website of the International Academy for Marital Spirituality, INTAMS, http://www.intams.org/Bishops Synod.htm.

CATHOLIC FAMILIES

Theology, Reality, and the Gospel

LISA SOWLE CAHILL

Pope Francis's decision to address the family with two special synods reflects the accurate perception that "family" can signify quite different realities globally. Catholic theology and pastoral ministry have not kept up with recent changes in family structure and social roles. Moreover, Catholic theology tends to conflate family and marriage. This article will consider some realities of family life, contributions and limits of Catholic theology, and possible new directions signaled by Pope Francis.

CATHOLIC THEOLOGY OF THE FAMILY

Three sources for contemporary family theology are Scripture, Catholic social teaching, and Catholic moral theology. Before crafting a theology of family, we need to establish what family is, relating it to yet distinguishing it from marriage. In the social sciences, "the family...is a social unit created by blood, marriage, or adoption, and can be described as nuclear (parents and children) or extended (encompassing other relatives)."[1] Families may or may not include marriage, but what they always involve are intergenerational parent-child relationships extended into kinship networks. How does Catholicism view families, understood as such networks?

A fundamental source for all Christian theology is *the Bible*. In the Hebrew Bible or Christian Old Testament, family is multigenerational, patriarchal, and polygamous, focused on producing heirs and descendants. Jesus' ministry of the reign of God decouples family identity and religious identity, loosening hierarchies within the family, and emphasizing the inclusive new "family" in Christ (Gal 3:28–29; Heb 2:10–11). The authentically Christian family is an open kin network, practicing love, hospitality, and service. *Catholic social teaching*'s message to families is to respect human dignity, justice, and mutual rights and duties, taking care, especially for "the least of these" (Matt 25:40).

The perspective on family of *Catholic moral theology* must be radically rethought before it can "move forward" as useable tradition today. One big problem is the confusion of family and marriage. A related problem is defining acceptable Catholic marriage in terms of the sacramentally valid, monogamous, permanent, procreative union of one man and one woman. Catholic theology consequently regards families as either good and respectable, or as deviant and "irregular," based upon the marital status and sexual acts of a couple heading the family. This is completely backward. An irregular *marriage* does not equate to an irregular *family*.

What constitutes *family* is not the married couple, but parent-child relationships, extending backward and forward in time, in the form of ancestors and descendants, and kin groups joined by marriages. A contemporary ethics of family should be concerned with the justice and the supportive nature of inter-generational relationships, not primarily with approved or dis-approved sex. In such a perspective, the moral-theological criteria of family would include "love and union" as mutuality, self-gift, and faithfulness among family members; "procreation" as the creation and education of the next generation, as well as care in old age for the previous procreative generation, and social concern for nonfamily members.

PRACTICES OF FAMILIES

In the United States and Western Europe, cohabitation increasingly competes with marriage as a way of forming sexual and domestic partnerships and of extending family relationships through childbearing. Today a growing number of families creates new generations outside legal marriage. The frameworks of procreative sex in marriage and nuclear households do not capture the reality of these families. European and North American societies may be undergoing a transition in the way sexual, domestic, and reproductive partnerships are formed. The question is what forms and patterns of relationship best serve the ability of families to care for their members, including the elderly and the young, and to contribute to society. The relevant variable in children's outcomes is not the family structure itself (or at least not alone) so much as "public policies which comparatively advantage certain family structures over others."[2]

How do Catholic laity experience these new realities? There are several areas of what Catholic ethicist Julie Clague calls "disjuncture" between official expectations and Catholic practices of marriage and family.[3] According to the minority of bishops who made public the results of the preparatory questionnaire for the 2014 synod, there is a significant divide between the laity and Church teachings on contraception, cohabitation, and divorce. Many Catholics seek greater pastoral understanding and flexibility toward same-sex couples, the remarried, and their children.[4] Most Catholic women use contraception, and many couples turn to in vitro fertilization to have families, even though it is forbidden by official teaching—a fact of which many are not even aware. There are no precise statistics on the number of Catholic couples who cohabit before or without marriage, but the fact that cohabitation is no longer seen as a barrier to marriage or to marriage preparation in the Catholic Church is an indicator that it is widely practiced and tolerated if not encouraged.

EVANGELIZATION: THEOLOGY, PRACTICES, AND PASTORAL RESPONSE

How can the Church or churches bring a message of hope, encouragement, consolation, and joy to families today? Let me propose three models for consideration, all of which are operative in proposals evoked by the synods.

The first centers on Pope Francis's watchword, *mercy*— connoting compassion, understanding, and acceptance for those who have broken valid rules. The second follows the virtue of equity or *epikeia*, described by Cardinal Walter Kasper as "a realistic application of doctrine to the current situation of the great majority of people."[5] A third, more radical approach would be to change specific Catholic teachings about sex, marriage, and the family. Certain core values may never change— such as the importance of marital commitment, sexual fidelity, and responsibility for children—but the rules derived from and protecting these values might. Examples—certainly quite far from any present *magisterial* recognition—are accepting gay marriage, divorce in certain cases, artificial birth control, or cohabitation as a morally valid form of union.

For Francis, it is vital to celebrate the grace in life before condemning what is "irregular" or a failure, and perhaps even to defer or forego judgment in favor of invitation and encouragement. Francis appreciates that in terms of ecclesial culture, politics, and moral-cultural outlooks, we are still feeling our way forward, a process the synods are meant to enable. The appropriate adaptation to today's family realities can be better discerned, and perhaps only discerned, once a climate of neighborly empathy has replaced the righteous judgment that too often and lamentably affects both or all "sides" of the family ethics disputes. Families are sometimes, for all of us, places where we bear the cross, and pray that Jesus will be in solidarity with us so that we can survive. But families, in their many forms and with all their sorrows, are also places of forgiveness, hope, and resurrection to new life after struggle. As Francis shows, this is the heart of the gospel for Christian families.

NOTES

1. Charles B. Nam, "The Concept of the Family: Demographic and Genealogical Approaches," *Sociation Today* 2, no. 2 (Fall 2004), http://www.ncsociology.org/sociationtoday /v22/family.htm.

2. Shelley Burtt, "What Children Really Need: Toward a Critical Theory of Family Structure," in *The Moral and Political Status of Children*, ed. David Archard and Colin Macleod (Oxford: Oxford University Press, 2002), 238.

3. See Julie Clague, "Catholics, Families, and the Synod of Bishops: Views from the Pews," *The Heythrop Journal*, 55, no. 6 (November 2014): 985–1008.

4. Julie Hanlon Rubio, "US Catholic Hopes for the Upcoming Synod on the Family," *INTAMS Review*, 20, no. 2 (2014): 13–18, at 13.

5. "Cardinal Walter Kasper's 'Gospel of the Family,'" Vatican Radio, March 10, 2014, http://www.news.va/en/news/cardinal-walter-kaspers-gospel-of-the-family.

THE LOVE THAT CROSSES LINES

The Graced Transgressions of Family Life

CLARE WATKINS

"It's no longer sustainable to claim that messed up lives are bad."
"There's a need to disentangle holiness from perfection."

**Voices from Catholic families, gathered
in the Listening 2004 project of the
Catholic Bishops' Conference
of England & Wales.**[1]

Peter said, "By no means, Lord; for I have never eaten anything that is profane or unclean."...
Peter was greatly puzzled about what to make of the vision that he had seen.

(Acts 10:14, 17)

If there is one question that has the power to renew our understanding for today's mission, it is this: "What *is* church teaching?" I don't mean, "What does the Church teach?" Rather, I'm posing a more fundamental question about the nature of that teaching and learning that enables fallen, often damaged, people, in their messy contexts, to grow in holiness.

Traditionally the Church understands herself as "teacher and mother." It is through my own "maternal thinking,"[2] as well as theological learning, that I want to reflect on "church teaching" and the learning toward holiness of ordinary Catholic families. I say "ordinary," but these families are often quite extraordinary in their wisdom and love, and frequently include the non-Catholic, the non-Christian, the nonfaithful. This essay acknowledges the human reality and Christian mystery that the home is the first school of faith (*CCC* 1657), and invites the whole Church to enter this school—in all its realities, imperfections, and mess—in order to hear magisterial teaching afresh. After all, "realities are greater than ideas" (*EG* 233).

What is church teaching? Mothers know that children need to be *taught*—about manners, sharing, and self-control, as well as through more formal education. Truthfully, though, these are the tip of the iceberg of domestic "teaching," which begins before a child is born, and continues through the loving (or unloving) relationships of family life. What maternal reasoning knows well is that you *directively* teach neither very young infants, nor (if you are wise) your young adult children. Here the "lessons" are first of all of unconditional love and total care, and subsequently of enabling independence, mutual respect, and the loving of one who has grown away, grown different, from ourselves.

As parents we know this—it is our bread-and-butter wisdom. So I wonder why we persistently hear the teaching of our Mother Church as the handing down of rules. It is as if our modern church culture has experienced a failure to understand what teaching and learning are for mature baptized people. If it has, then this is a failure of its maternal wisdom.

To locate ourselves in the "domestic church" is to be in the place where "rules" are instinctively seen as a tiny and occasionally necessary part of a deeper learning of love, compassion, self-giving, and humility. This ordinary family wisdom comes to the fore when it is tested by the movement into difference that is part of healthy maturing. As our children learn, quite properly, to become "other" to their parents and siblings, there can be painful challenges, not simply to "rules" but more significantly to the unspoken assumptions about how relationships are carried out in the home.

These ordinary moments of growth and challenge are acutely represented in those common instances where a Catholic family faces situations that are felt to be "transgressive" in some way: when an adult child chooses to live with their partner rather than marry; when your son or daughter identifies as gay or lesbian, and seeks acceptance for their partner into the family; when your child's unhappy marriage ends in divorce and they find happiness with another spouse; when your teenage child questions their own gender and seeks gender transition. To describe these experiences as experiences of (among other things) "transgression" is not, for me, a moral statement; rather, it identifies moments that go against hitherto accepted rules or norms, moments where a *line is crossed*.

In my own context, as a Catholic in England, I can think of not one Catholic family, in all the churches I have known and worked with, which has not included some such moments of crossing a line. This fact is important. It means that each time a bishop sends a pastoral letter on same-sex marriage, or divorce and remarriage, into parishes, and each time a priest repeats rules about eucharistic discipline in these areas, tender places in the hearts of *every* family are touched, often painfully. The lines that have been crossed are clearly drawn, and the transgressive experiences of each family silently grieved over. But that is not the whole story.

For the maternal heart knows that it is truly painful to see one's children's marriages break down, or to see them struggling with sexual identity and their faith; *and* it is humanly joyful to see their brokenness transformed by the love of a new spouse, or a committed partner. The maternal heart is able to carry a certain bewilderment—resonant with the Marian pondering heart of Luke 2—in which a faithful belief in the indissolubility of marriage goes hand in hand with a delighted embrace of the second wife, the step-family, and all the complexity of blended families. Her faith as such hasn't *changed*—

the rule still speaks of something profound and deeply truth-ful—but in her receiving of the son's male partner she discov-ers, with a gasp, the extraordinary power of a love that can cross lines and be made greater and stronger in that journey. Here some of the most profound parental learning takes place, as we see new possibilities and ways of blessing unfolded in our chil-dren's lives, even "beyond the line."

These are the lessons I have learned in my own parental living of faith, and through the testimony of innumerable Catholic families. When these households of faith (and doubt) are given voice, we most often encounter this witness to grace in the apparently transgressive. As one contributor to the *Listening 2004* project puts it,

> If your children as adults make choices that are not in line with the Church's traditional teaching it is a challenge for you and the Church. You cannot turn off your love for your children and I think you have to accept their choices even if they're not your choices for them. I think we as parents can teach the Church something about real love here.

It's not that we Catholic parents disagree, simply, with Church teaching. It is rather that the mysterious love we practice *as parents* has compelled us into crossing the line; and what we can-not deny is that, in these moments of transgression, we have experienced a profundity of compassion, grace, and peace.

All this is, of course, risky. I write it without any great claims to attach to it, and quite simply as a testimony to mater-nal love and wisdom. However, I can't end without reflecting that discovering grace through the transgressive act of crossing the line is not so very alien to the Christian tradition. The Petrine office, as a universal office of unity, is rooted in the struggle against the Spirit's pushing the Church over a certain line. In "Peter's Halakhic nightmare"[3] of Acts 10, we surely see nothing less than the transgressive move as a graced move toward opening up the future to new life. For those many, many families who feel they have crossed the line and been surprised by *grace*, the questions inexorably emerge, as they did, perhaps, of Peter, puzzled by what they have seen: Where did this line come from? Who taught us that there was a line there anyway? And what have we learned beyond the keeping of the rule?

And, now I think of it, it surely wasn't *lines* Jesus drew in the sand (cf. John 8:1–11); but whatever it was, it led to the adulterous woman's escaping the due punishment, and being forgiven—freed.

NOTES

1. *Not Easy but Full of Meaning: Catholic Family Life in 2004; A Report of the Findings of Listening 2004; My Family My Church*, Catholic Bishops' Conference of England and Wales, at http://www.cbcew.org.uk/marriage-and-family-life.

2. See Sara Ruddick, *Maternal Thinking. Towards a Politics of Peace* (New York: Ballantine Books, 1989).

3. See John R. L. Moxon, *Peter's Halakhic Nightmare: Acts 10:9–16 in Jewish and Graeco-Roman Perspective* (Tubingen: Mohr Siebeck, forthcoming).

WHAT ON EARTH CAN COMPLEMENTARITY ACTUALLY BE?

SARA MAITLAND

Every year, on International Women's Day and other such occasions, the media does the old dreary plod through the numbers to see that inequality between the sexes continues across almost every conceivable measure: women in global and national statistics do less well in health, wealth, basic freedoms and rights, and access to education, to chosen employment, to leisure, to safety, and to respect. Accounts of rape and violence against women should be far more shocking than they are, but we all know that many men (and some women) still believe that women are responsible for their own rapes and that often they were "asking for it."

And what is Holy Mother Church doing about it? Burbling on about "complementarity," without even acknowledging that there are obvious problems—theological, ethical, and observational—with the concept itself.

Pope Francis sometimes only adds to the confusion when he tries to justify the concept. For example, in an address to a 2014 colloquium on the topic he said, "When we speak of complementarity between man and woman..., let us not confuse that term with the simplistic idea that all the roles and relations of the two sexes are fixed in a single, static pattern.

This is an edited version of an article that first appeared in *The Tablet* on March 12, 2015—reproduced with permission of the publisher: http://www.thetablet.co.uk/.

Complementarity will take many forms as each man and woman brings his or her distinctive contributions to their marriage and to the formation of their children."[1]

If that is the case, then it is hard to see why complementarity should not apply to two people of the same sex; but more importantly here, if there is not a "single static pattern" leading joyfully to specific roles, then what on earth can complementarity actually be? It cannot, obviously, subsist simply in the biological facts of reproduction, because that would mean that at any given moment over 50 percent of women in the world were not "real" women (too old, too young, or infertile). If we are just saying all people are unique individuals, then fine, but that hardly constitutes some mysterious abstract that makes all women fitted for nurturing and men for leadership.

If complementarity is not a concrete something that manifests itself anywhere, we are pushed back on to a language of "nature" (usually "women's nature" or "femininity"). But as soon as we start thinking that there are two different natures, however complementary, then we are in serious trouble— because in the incarnation, Jesus assumed human nature and it is through that assumption of our nature that we are redeemed. If we want to say there are two different natures, then the whole paradigm of salvation collapses, and women are not saved. I am sure there is a cunning theological solution to this, but no one is even acknowledging that there might be some doctrinal issues here—complementarity is treated as obvious, a default position, and if a few hysterical feminists would just rid themselves of the virus of "gender ideology" everything would be well.

But it is not well and it cannot be well. Through all of history and across all known societies in one form or another (and the forms vary enormously), gender stereotyping and an ideology of unthought-through "natural" complementarity has prevailed; and nowhere, ever, has it led to equality, and always, everywhere, women have been the sufferers. "Equal but different" and "separate development" is the rhetoric of apartheid, of segregation, and of violence. Is it really imaginable that God can have devised a plan, or will endorse a way of being, that is consistently incapable of delivering justice to more than half the human beings in the world?

I think it would be a good thing if we, as Church, admitted that there was a justice issue as well as a philosophical problem about gender and its meanings. We could then stop sneering at those people (usually feminists) who are trying to reconfigure gender, and search for a better way of describing differences between individuals and struggle to create a more just world. Remember the geocentric universe? Matthean primacy? Sometimes we get things wrong.

Perhaps we could start by appointing a saint for feminists and make her feast day International Women's Day—just as St. Joseph the Worker was moved to May Day in 1955 in response to the Communists' celebrations. I'm nominating Radegund because she left an abusive husband, was made a deacon, worked for peace, and insisted that her nuns had proper academic study time. Other suggestions welcome.

NOTE

1. "Pope Francis's Address at Opening of Colloquium on Complementarity of Man and Woman," November 17, 2014, at http://www.zenit.org/en/articles/pope-francis-address-at-opening-of-colloquium-on-complementarity-of-man-and-woman.

SAINT ANNE: A SAINT FOR TODAY?

A Reflection on Grandmothers and Holy Families

TINA BEATTIE

I did my doctoral research on the theology and symbolism of the Virgin Mary when my four children were very young. I was motivated by a personal as well as a theological interest in the Mother of God. I had converted to Catholicism from a Presbyterian background soon after the birth of my youngest child, and I was gradually experiencing a transformation in my Christian faith. After the austere scriptural focus of the Calvinist tradition, I was discovering the lush sacramentality of a tradition that recognizes the grace of God glistening within the material world, transforming mundane realities into sacramental signs and rituals refulgent with the mystery of the divine.

During my PhD I engaged closely with the work of Luce Irigaray, who brings feminist philosophical and theological insights to her reading of Lacanian psychoanalysis.[1] Irigaray interprets Freud's theory of the Oedipus complex, with its account of a violent infantile trauma of separation from the maternal body, as an insight into the dynamics that have shaped our Western understanding of nature and embodiment. She sees Freud's theory as reinforcing a dualistic ethos that privileges rationality, abstraction, and transcendence over desire, embodiment, and immanence. The result is a culture of negation and denial, of contempt for the female body, as well as contempt for nature because of the long association between woman and nature.

In her quest for positive representations of the maternal relationship—and particularly of the mother-daughter relationship that barely features in Christian theology and psychoanalytic theory—Irigaray frequently refers to Mary and also to her mother, St. Anne, who was a popular focus of late medieval devotion. This awakened in me an enduring interest in the cult of St. Anne and, having recently become a grandmother myself, I now turn to her as a neglected but rich resource for prayer and reflection.

Anne (or Anna) first appears in the second-century apocryphal text, the *Protevangelium of James*,[2] which tells of Mary's early life. She is modeled on the Old Testament figure of Hannah, mother of Samuel. Like Hannah, Anne is an elderly woman who laments her lack of children. While most traditional cultures blame the woman when a marriage is childless, in the *Protevangelium* Anne's husband, Joachim, exiles himself to the desert to fast and pray because of his failure to father a child. In a scene that echoes the annunciation, an angel appears simultaneously to Anne in mourning at home, and to Joachim in the wilderness. The angel tells Joachim to return home, for they are to have a child. Anne rushes to meet him and they fall into one another's arms at the city gate. This loving marital embrace, known as the "Kiss at the Golden Gate," represented the conception of the Virgin in late medieval art.[3] However, at the Council of Trent such images were discouraged lest they arouse concupiscence in the faithful, perhaps because Church teaching never denied that Mary was sexually conceived: after that embrace Anne and Joachim went home and had sex. Spanish artists subsequently developed the iconography of the immaculate conception that is more familiar to us today.

Alongside this beautiful depiction of married love, the cult of St. Anne inspired tender images of the mother-daughter relationship. When Mary is born, Anne declares her joy on learning that the child is female. Even today, in many cultures the birth of a daughter is seen as a burden rather than a blessing, so this is a rare and maybe even unique account of a mother's cry of joy at her daughter's birth. Images of Anne teaching Mary to read offer a representation of female literacy that defies stereotypical ideas about women in the Middle Ages.[4] Many paintings and sculptures show Anne with the Virgin and Christ. These are known as "Anne Trinitarian" or *Anna Selbdritt*, expressing the popular belief that, while the heavenly Trinity comprises Christ, the Holy Spirit, and God the Father, the earthly Trinity was the incarnate Jesus, his mother, and his grandmother.[5] With the gradual eclipse of St. Anne in the transition from the Middle Ages to the Catholic Reformation and modernity, St. Joseph took the place of St. Anne in this holy family grouping of the earthly Trinity.[6]

An even more fascinating genre of late medieval art is the "Holy Kinship" group. This is ascribed to stories about the saints in the popular collection known as *The Golden Legend*, which gave rise to the tradition known as the *trinubium*, or three marriages of Anne.[7] Seeking to explain references to the brothers and sisters of Jesus in the Gospels, the legend told that after the death of Joachim, Anne was married twice more, once to Cleopas and once to Salome, and each of these marriages resulted in another daughter—the women referred to in the Gospels as Mary Cleopas and Mary Salome. There is a vast array of medieval images showing the Holy Kinship—St. Anne as a matriarchal figure seated among her three daughters and their children, with the Virgin beside her and Christ held between them.

Such images earthed the story of Christ in the domestic realities of women's lives. However, the Reformation and Catholic Reformation sought in different ways to distance themselves from what were perceived as the excesses and superstitions of these nonscriptural medieval devotions. As a result, St. Anne has little relevance for most Christians today, though she is patron saint of numerous causes and regions, including Quebec and Brittany, and she remains a significant figure in Orthodox liturgy.

The cult of St. Anne expresses a deep insight about the incarnation that is relevant for us today. Christ was born into a community of women, with aunts and a grandmother who participated in his care. Today, in sub-Saharan Africa, grandmothers are often the key figures who hold families together, caring for children orphaned by AIDS. Research has shown that infant mortality is affected by the absence or presence of the maternal grandmother. When a poor woman's mother is present, her children are more likely to survive.[8]

These images also show us that there are many ways of being a holy family. The modern image of the Holy Family as Mary, Joseph, and Jesus replaced those extended matriarchal kinship groups of late medieval Catholicism, reflecting but also shaping widespread changes in cultural perceptions of what it means to be a family. Today, the family is once again changing, with the breakdown of the modern nuclear family, with divorce and remarriage, and with changing patterns of cohabitation and parenting. The nuclear family emerged within a particular economic and social context—namely, the modern Western capitalist state. As that political ideology disintegrates, the family structure that sustained it is also disintegrating. Instead of lamenting, we might look to the past to discover how to imagine new ways of being family and raising children, and we might ask St. Anne, God's grandmother, to pray for us.

NOTES

1. See Tina Beattie, *God's Mother, Eve's Advocate: A Marian Narrative of Women's Salvation* (New York: Continuum, 2002).

2. Links to the Greek text and several English translations of the *Protevangelium of the Gospel of James* can be found at the website Early Christian Writings, http://www.earlychristianwritings. com/infancyjames.html.

3. A search on Google Images will produce a range of such images. One of the earliest and most famous is that of Giotto di Bondone (c. 1305), in the Arena Chapel in Padua.

4. Again, a Google search will produce an abundance of such medieval images.

5. Cf. Pamela Sheingorn, "Appropriating the Holy Kinship" in *Interpreting Cultural Symbols: Saint Anne in Late Medieval Society*, ed. Kathleen Ashley and Pamela Sheingorn (Athens, GA: The University of Georgia Press, 1994), 169–98.

6. Cf. Bartolomé Esteban Murillo, *The Heavenly and Earthly Trinities* (1675–82), National Gallery, London.

7. See Virginia Nixon, *Mary's Mother: Saint Anne in Late Medieval Europe* (University Park, PA: Pennsylvania State University Press, 2004).

8. Cf. Rebecca Sear and Ruth Mace, "Who Keeps Children Alive? A Review of the Effects of Kin on Child Survival," *Evolution and Human Behavior* 29, no.1 (January 2008): 1–18.

WELCOME BUT NOT WELCOME

Going to Mass with My Baptist Husband

MARGARET WATSON

I was baptized in the Anglican Church as a child and brought up to go to church, but it meant little to me until I came to personal faith at the age of eighteen. A friend took me through Romans 3:22–23—"There is no distinction, since all have sinned and fall short of the glory of God"—so I acknowledged my sin. Then she led me to Romans 6:23—"The free gift of God is eternal life in Christ Jesus our Lord." Finally we looked at John 3:16 and she asked me to put my name in place of "the world," so I read, "For God so loved Margaret that he gave his only Son, so that if she believes in him she will not perish but may have eternal life."

At that time I was just starting my training as a nurse. Later I did my midwifery training with the Salvation Army, and then trained to be an officer, being ordained in 1978. I had a number of appointments, including leading churches, before going out to Pakistan to run a health center.

Some years later I met my husband, also a Christian, while we were both working as missionaries in the Himalayas. We have been married for over thirty years. For a number of years we attended the Baptist church together, where John was a deacon. Then about five years ago God led me, to my great surprise, toward the Catholic Church, and I was confirmed into membership at Pentecost two years ago.

My problem is inconsistency regarding whether or not my husband is allowed to receive communion when we go to Mass together. If we are away from home we tend to go to Roman Catholic churches. We explain that my husband is a believer but not a Catholic, and he has always been allowed to participate in the Mass. This however seems to depend upon the attitude of the local priest rather than any fixed rule. In the parish I now live in England, he would be refused, despite the fact that he is known and respected as a Christian worker by the priests concerned. We rely on visiting priests as we have no regular parish priest, but the general attitude seems to be, "We must keep the rules of the Church," to which my reply is, "What about the urging of the Holy Spirit?"

I believe that Christ accepts us both because we believe in him as our Savior, and I find I can no longer attend a Mass where my beloved husband is excluded. He is a man of great faith, and there will be no labels in heaven.

We have discussed John's becoming a Catholic. There is no pressure on my side, but he raises the subject from time to time. However, this would be almost entirely to help me to feel better about a Church which excludes him, and I do not believe that this is a good reason.

I believe the message of the Gospels is clear. God loves us all, even with our many faults. He does not want exclusion, but inclusion. I recently attended a local Mass that included a baptism, so there were a number of visitors. The priest explained that those who were practicing Catholics could take the elements, but that those who were not Catholic or who were Catholic but were for some reason prevented from full participation, should simply come forward for a blessing. He had earlier welcomed us all to the service, but when the time came for communion maybe a third of the people stayed in their seats. Welcome, but not welcome. So sad and destructive.

MARRIAGE AND DIVORCE: TELLING OUR STORIES

Marriage and Divorce through the Eyes of a Child

ALISON CONCANNON KENNEDY

Martin's mother was a saint, he told me. To her children Marian personified all the qualities of the saints she had encouraged them to emulate: an unselfish, humble, and holy woman whom they were proud to call "Mother," alone in her parental commitment to their faith. Her husband, their father, was a nominal Catholic who had numerous affairs, occasionally going to Mass with the family to sit alongside his wife and seven children, receiving holy communion from a priest who, at the end of the celebration, was proud to shake the hand of this seemingly devout father. The marriage ended in divorce when, after thirty-five years, their father left the family home to marry one of his long-standing conquests. Only with the inno- cence of childhood behind them did the children begin to truly see the pain and humiliation of their mother.

Later, Martin and his siblings watched a good man's love and friendship bring about much-needed healing for their mother, wiping the hidden tears, encouraging laughter and a growing self-worth. But her commitment to the new relation- ship and subsequent registry office marriage brought about another pain, the pain of excommunication, which was to deeply challenge the seeds of faith that Marian's dedicated nur- turing had planted in her children. The children saw their mother, responsible for all that was good in their lives, continue to attend Mass every Sunday, not able to approach the altar and receive the food of life that she had so reverently introduced to them as children.

Today, none of Marian's children consider themselves Catholic. Their mother had shown them a God of love, but the Catholic Church had witnessed to them a God of rules and regulations, lacking compassion and mercy in holding her to the unreciprocated wedding-day promise.

I am also a Catholic divorcee, having been married for twenty-seven years. When I married at twenty I made a promise that I intended to honor "until death do us part," but death happened gradually and in a way I did not expect. We were both young, swept away by the romance of our differing worlds and, for the sake of peace, I found my faith had to fade into the background—and a part of me died.

When children came, motherhood required me to revisit the steps of faith that had been so much part of who I was—baptism, Mass, Catholic schools, first holy communion, confirmation—and I realized my Catholic faith could no longer be denied. For my husband the renewed expression of my faith became an even greater obstacle than at the beginning of the marriage, a conflict of beliefs that eventually killed both of us emotionally, leading to irretrievable breakdown in our relationship. Then, in answer to my prayer, he met somebody who could fulfill what he wanted from a wife and we had a fairly amicable divorce. I am very grateful for our children and proud of the caring adults they have become. However, I am saddened that they have rejected the rich heritage and goodness of faith I'd tried to share, their adult reasoning seeing the Church as responsible for the pain and unhappiness of the family home.

Pastoral care of Catholics going through divorce is a lottery, dependent on the strengths and sympathies of the individual priest. There is no Church-recognized ministry that walks alongside divorcing Catholics and it is a very lonely journey, often accompanied by cruel and unforgiving parish gossip from Catholic misconceptions.

My experience has given me empathy with many Catholics who have traveled that same route. I have shared their sad and painful stories of infidelity, of mental and physical cruelty, none of which could be justified by the promise "for better or worse." But the real sadness is that in many failed Catholic unions there are children watching, judging the Church as it judges their parents, impressionable witnesses to the cold stony path of the annulment process that a loved parent is forced along, with no guarantee of success.

I look for guidance on marriage in the Scriptures and I find passages in Mark (10:2–12) and Matthew (19:3–10), where Jesus is asked by the Pharisees and later his disciples to affirm the understanding of the law of Moses on divorce and marriage, quotations used to justify the Church's indissolubility of marriage. I read in the verses that follow both accounts, "Let the little children come...," and with sadness reflect on how many little children, descendants of those unforgiven spouses, have been lost to the Church. I think of my friend, Martin, and his six siblings, all now in their fifties and sixties, and their children and grandchildren—three generations of one family. I think of my own children and grandchildren....

I do not know whether Marian was allowed communion on her deathbed, but I do believe that she has received the forgiveness and acceptance, due to her by her Church, when, as a child of God, she was welcomed into the arms of her loving Creator.

MARRIAGE AND DIVORCE: TELLING OUR STORIES

Traumatic Divorce and Sacramental Healing

PIPPA BONNER

Between 1991 and 1996 I was divorced, my marriage was annulled, I went through the Internal Forum and was remarried. My first marriage lasted twenty years and I have been married to my second husband for eighteen years. During those early years in the 1990s I was looking after three teenage children, working almost full-time and studying part-time for a master's in theology and religious studies. I now realize I got through the last years of my first marriage with sadness and determination, trying to attend to the needs of my children and also retaining some energy for my job with social work clients.

I had expected to be married to my first husband for life, and I tried to keep everything together. However, his alcoholism and the discovery that he had been spending all our money made me realize that I had to make some decisions for the sake of the children. He was not abusive but his drinking, mood swings, and unreliability meant that his children lost their respect for him, and his capacity to care for them became unpredictable. The crisis came when I discovered that our house had secretly been put up for collateral, and only emergency money from my mother-in-law prevented us from becoming homeless. Also, my children and their friends had amazingly survived a car crash caused by his drunk driving. I believed I had to divorce to protect our children and control enough of the family income to keep us going.

After our divorce I sought and obtained an annulment. A few years later I met my second husband. He was also divorced but, as he was not a Catholic, I could not expect him to go through an annulment. Without this, theoretically I would not be able to receive communion, so I went to a priest to ask about the Internal Forum. This is a private forum of conscience, involving discussion with a priest and absolution. Not many priests know about it. I spoke to the priest about my situation and within an hour he told me that I was free to receive communion. It was a simple but graced experience and a compassionate solution for me. I understand that Pope John Paul II did not wish it to be widely used.

My second husband later decided to become a Catholic and obtained an annulment, as our parish priest at the time required it. Having initially had a registry office wedding and a blessing from my parish priest, after my husband's annulment we finally had a nuptial mass.

That was many years ago. I believe that, if I had had the confidence, healing, and security I experience now, I might not have gone down the annulment route with all the complications that followed. I might have become one of the one-third of divorced and remarried Catholics who present themselves "unannulled" for communion, in good conscience.[1] Or, I might have drifted away from the Church, hurt and with a chip on my shoulder, which left unhealed would have become more painful over time.

To restore the Internal Forum would be a pastoral response to the painful dilemmas facing Catholics in situations similar to my own. Sacraments are healing. Divorce is traumatic for everyone concerned, but it is sometimes the only solution for the well-being of the spouse and the protection of children.

Divorced and remarried Catholics are being denied communion at a time of change and vulnerability. Pope Francis seeks a collegial Church of compassion. The Internal Forum is based on conscience, discernment, and openness to mercy. The institutional Church needs to trust laypeople and priests with their bishops, to allow informed conscience and discernment to come to a sacramental conclusion that keeps the Eucharist at the heart of the Church.

NOTES

1. See Catherine Pepinster, "Bestriding the World," *The Tablet*, May 16, 2015, 8.

MARRIAGE AND DIVORCE: TELLING OUR STORIES

A Very Faithful Rebel

ANNA CANNON

I probably hold a world record in speed marrying, or rather speed deciding to say yes to a marriage offer. It took all of nineteen-and-a-half hours from the moment I first set eyes on my husband-to-be to him proposing and me accepting. And did we live happily ever after? You bet we did not.

This whirlwind romance happened in Poland, my native country. I was in my late twenties, single, with a master's degree in English, working in a desirable job, with no plans to leave either the job or the country. My husband-to-be was British, also an English graduate. We married as soon as the necessary paperwork allowed—with one registry and one church wedding (Catholic, with a special dispensation—my husband was a baptized but nonpracticing Anglican), but with absolutely no marriage preparation offered by the Church, apart from having to promise that any children would be brought up in the Catholic faith. I joined my husband in England within a few months.

That "Church-approved" marriage lasted four profoundly damaging years, in which I was exposed to mental cruelty and abuse as well as serial infidelity, and ended six months after our daughter was born. During that time, although practicing my faith was on the back burner, I knew that I would never leave it. The stimulus to return to being a practicing Catholic came when I became pregnant and realized I was going to be responsible for another person's soul. I marveled at the astonishing privilege of motherhood, which gives a woman a chance to be so intimately involved with God in the miracle and the mystery of creation. This was much deeper than any teaching learned in catechism classes. It is a matter of being connected to God in the deepest core of my being.

After my husband left us, I found myself on my own with a young child in a country that was not my own (stubborn pride prevented me from going back to my parents), and lived in relative poverty and misery for the next three years, until I found an ideal job with a salary that put an end to any money worries. I bought a house, and soon acquired a circle of new friends through work. There I met the man who eventually became my second husband.

Apart from falling in love with each other, which was the easiest part, the situation was not straightforward at all. My partner was and remains a firm nonbeliever, although baptized Polish Orthodox and respectful of my faith; I was a divorcée whose Catholic faith had been reawakened with pregnancy and childbirth. When we began living together I stopped receiving communion, though I still regularly attended Mass and sang in our church choir.

We sent my daughter to a Catholic primary school, where she was prepared for her first communion. She soon started asking why I did not receive communion with her. It was, spiritually, a very difficult and painful time for me because of the impossibility of squaring the formal requirements of my religion with how I was living my life—even though my relationship with my partner was one of love, commitment, friendship, and mutual trust and fidelity.

My dilemma was eventually resolved thanks to meeting a wise and compassionate confessor. In the end, I was able to receive the sacraments again, and we continued living together as a family. We brought up my daughter together, and my partner was the best father I could wish for her. Like any married couple, our relationship had its ups and downs but we were there for each other through all the responsibilities and demands of family life. In my parish, I trained to be a reader and eucharistic minister.

Finally, after nearly thirty years of being together, my partner and I decided to formalize our relationship. We married in a civil ceremony three years ago. I laughed that, after my first disastrously precipitate decision to marry, it took thirty years to finally decide I could trust my fiancé enough to tie the knot. Three months after the civil marriage, we received a blessing on our union from our parish priest who came to the conclusion, based on his conscience and within the provisions of canon law, that there were enough grounds to consider my first marriage invalid even without a formal church annulment.

Our marriage is by no means perfect, but we have thirty-three years of being together to keep us going. My first marriage, although formally contracted in church as a sacrament, was far from having any sacramental grace, whereas my second relationship has been everything that a genuinely sacramental union involves, despite not being officially recognized by the Church for more than thirty years. Even now that it has been blessed in a church ceremony by my parish priest, this is not the same as it being officially endorsed in terms of canon law.

My faith and commitment to a relationship with God is strengthening, maturing, and evolving all the time, though my conscience obliges me to question some of the Church's dogmas and magisterial dictates. I'm glad that, with the help of compassionate, wise, and open-minded priests and confessors, I have been able to remain "in the fold," though I tend to describe myself, paradoxically, as a very faithful rebel.

MARRIAGE, SEXUALITY, AND CONTRACEPTION

Natural Law, Moral Discernment, and the Authority of the Church

JEAN PORTER

When we speak of a natural-law account of Christian marriage, we must take note of those aspects of human nature that this account privileges, while at the same time attending to the theological commitments underlying it. In particular, this account does imply a normative link between sexuality and procreation, but it also embodies other ideals and commitments, not necessarily related to sexuality per se, that must also be taken into consideration. These commitments, in turn, provide the context within which to assess Christian teachings and practices on contraception.

The Christian understanding of marriage and procreation implies that there is something problematic about the use of contraceptives. If procreation is a human good, and if we have serious doctrinal reasons for insisting on this teaching and incorporating it into our common life, then it seems to follow that there is something incongruous from the Christian standpoint in the use of contraceptives. This incongruity helps to account for what otherwise would be hard to understand, namely, why it is that we within the Christian community

Edited extract from Jean Porter, "Contraceptive Use and the Authority of the Church: A Case Study on Natural Law and Moral Discernment" in *A Just and True Love*, ed. Maura Ryan and Brian Linnane (University of Notre Dame Press, 2008): 369-405.

identify the use of contraceptives as a moral issue at all and why we find a consistent condemnation of the use of contraceptives throughout the history of Christian reflections on sexuality.

Yet none of this necessarily implies that this condemnation need be binding on us today. Indeed, it is by no means obvious that a strict prohibition on the use of contraceptives is necessary to preserve the fundamental Christian affirmation of the goodness of marriage and procreation. On the contrary, as many theologians have argued, there is a good case to be made that it is not.[1]

This brings us to the question of the status of the magisterium's teaching on the use of contraceptives. According to Germain Grisez and John Ford, the received Catholic teaching on contraceptives meets the criteria set forth by Vatican II for an infallible teaching of the ordinary magisterium; that is to say, throughout history it has been taught by all Catholic bishops as something to be held definitively by all the faithful.[2] As they admit, this is to some extent an argument from silence. They consider it to be powerful nonetheless, since no one has yet offered a clear counterexample, in spite of the extensive study that this subject has received.

In response, Francis Sullivan asks what I think is the critical question: "How do they understand what it means to teach something as to be held definitively?"[3] As he goes on to observe, for them "definitive" seems to be equivalent to "binding in conscience," or sometimes, "scripturally based." The practical consequence of this view would be that every moral teaching of the ordinary magisterium is infallible; that is to say, the distinction between authoritative and infallible teachings would be rendered meaningless. This, in turn, would imply that the teachings of the magisterium can never develop in substantive ways, since once the magisterium has infallibly defined something, of course it cannot reverse itself later on. In Sullivan's view, such an interpretation is not consistent with the understanding of infallibility set forth in both Vatican Councils.[4]

It is perhaps obvious, but worth noting, that any attempt to apply Vatican II criteria for infallible teaching to earlier periods cannot be understood as a simple appeal to an objective matter of fact having to do with what "the Church has taught." In the process of applying these criteria, we are making an interpretive theological judgment about the significance of consensus (in the case at hand)—to say nothing of the further judgments that must be made in determining what counts as a consensus, who counts as the Church, and the like.

It has often been argued that a commitment to the good-ness of procreation and its integral place within marriage does not necessarily rule out the use of contraceptives. The evidence from the Scholastic period, limited though it is, seems to sup-port this conclusion, suggesting that in one period at least, the sinfulness of contraception was viewed as an implication, and not a centrally important implication, of certain views of sexu-ality and marriage. Given its reassessment of the sinful or prob-lematic character of sexual desire—a reassessment that itself began in this period—we can understand how the Christian community could qualify its views on the sinfulness of contra-ceptive use without thereby reversing its fundamental commit-ments to the good of marriage and procreation.[5]

Moreover, there is a case to be made that some acceptance of contraceptive use, within the context of an institutional com-mitment to both marriage and procreation, is actually necessary to safeguard other natural law commitments, which are arguably even more central to Christian moral practices, and which have also progressively transformed our understanding of marriage. Lisa Cahill points out that, given the conditions of modern industrialized society, the full equality of women both within marriage and within society as a whole requires some regulation of births, which can only practically be implemented through judicious use of contraceptives.[6] It would be easy to dismiss this as an attempt to challenge Church teachings by the standards of contemporary liberal values, but equality is itself a natural law ideal, and one that is central to Christian belief and practice. Given this, a judicious use of contraceptives, which respects the overall openness of the marital relation to children, can actually be a way of safeguarding and expressing the natural law in a contemporary context.

If this conclusion were to be adopted by the magisterium, would this amount to a reversal of a previously held moral teaching, and if so, what would be the implications of that fact? These issues cannot be explored here in any detail, but I would like to touch on them briefly, by way of conclusion.

First of all, the distinction between a reformulation or qualification of a previously held teaching, and its flat reversal, is not always clear. Much depends on just what one identifies as the teaching in question. If we consider the teaching in question to be the goodness of procreation and its centrality in Christian marriage, then it makes sense to say that by allowing for the licitness of contraceptive use we would be qualifying and extending a fundamental moral commitment in light of current circumstances, but not repudiating anything centrally important to a Christian understanding of marriage. Nonetheless, it is difficult to deny that such a move would involve a reversal of teaching at some level. Once we said that the use of contraceptives is always sinful; now we say that it is not. If this does not count as a reversal, what does?

We might ask this in the context of other teachings. For example, it is often said that the magisterium reversed itself on the question of usury, but this claim depends on a particular view of what counts as usury, namely, charging any interest at all (which is no longer condemned), as opposed to charging excessive interest (which is still condemned).

A clearer example, which is also more directly relevant to the question of contraceptive use, is the teaching on the marriage debt, that is to say, the obligation on the part of either partner to offer sex to the other on request.[7] This, it was said, is a grave obligation that can only be refused on penalty of serious sin. Not only was this a theological teaching, but the right to the marriage debt was defended in church courts. Yet we no longer speak of the marriage debt in these terms, or indeed in any terms, as far as I can determine. It is difficult to imagine any priest or counselor in a Catholic context telling someone that he or she has a serious obligation to offer sexual gratification to the spouse on demand; nor would this be likely to occur to most Catholic couples. We simply seem to have dropped the idea.

It might be said that this is not an example of a magisterial reversal; the magisterium never declared that the received teaching regarding the marital debt has now been canceled, it simply stopped mentioning it. To the best of my knowledge that is true, but then it is easy to imagine something similar happening in the case of the current teaching on contraceptive use. It is difficult to imagine that any future pope or council of bishops would explicitly repudiate this teaching, but it is easy to imagine, in fact it seems probable, that at some point in the near future the magisterium will just stop talking about it. This possibility does raise real theological problems, but these problems do not arise solely in the context of moral teaching.

Most Catholic theologians would agree that the Church, and by extension the magisterium, safeguards revelation and represents God's will in a definitive, or a paradigmatic, or an indispensable way. None of this implies, however, that it does so in a transparent way, free from all the limitations of its humanness. In order to fully address these problems it would be necessary to sort out the different ways in which these limitations affect the processes of ecclesial discernment and magisterial formulation, a worthy way to take this discussion further in the future.

NOTES

1. John Noonan is one such theologian. See John Noonan, *Contraception: A History of Its Treatment by the Catholic Theologians and Canonists* (Cambridge, MA: Harvard University Press, 1965; reprinted by New York: Mentor/Omega Books, 1967), 565–631.

2. Germain Grisez and John Ford, "Contraception and the Infallibility of the Ordinary Magisterium," *Theological Studies* 39 (1978): 258–312.

3. Francis A. Sullivan, *Magisterium: Teaching Authority in the Catholic Church* (Mahwah, NJ: Paulist Press, 1983), 145.

4. Ibid., 144–45.

5. To my knowledge, the first theologian to question the sinfulness of sexual desire is William of Auxerre (d. 1231) who claims that sexual delight would have existed in paradise, and should therefore be distinguished from sinful lust; see William of Auxerre, *Summa aurea* 17.1.1.

6. Lisa Cahill, *Sex, Gender and Christian Ethics* (Cambridge: Cambridge University Press, 1996), 201.

7. On the doctrine of the marriage debt, see Noonan, *Contraception*, 343–45; James Brundage, *Law, Sex and Christian Society in Medieval Europe* (Chicago: University of Chicago Press, 1987), 282–84, 358–60, 505–7.

CONSCIENCE AND CONTRACEPTION: TELLING OUR STORIES

Natural Family Planning: Sharing the Struggles

RACHEL ESPINOZA AND TAWNY HORNER

Pope Francis opened the 2014 synod of Bishops with a call for open discussion of challenges facing the family, yet transcripts of the testimonies given by the married couples who spoke at the synod reveal that there was only a cursory discussion of the challenges involved in couples' openness to life. Missing were the voices of Catholic couples who embrace church teaching on this issue but who struggle with ambiguous fertility signs, the marital strain of extended abstinence, the complications caused by medical conditions and poor finances, and even unplanned pregnancies, while following all the guidelines for their method of Natural Family Planning (NFP).

One woman expresses what such struggles entail when she says, "A few times I cried myself to sleep over my [NFP] chart with my dismayed husband, unsure how to help me. Sex wasn't an integral part of our sacramental love for each other; it was a rare treat that had to be compartmentalized." While abstinence can be a tool for learning discipline, selflessness, and communication,

Edited article reprinted from *America*, May 18, 2015, with permission of America Press, Inc. (2015). All rights reserved. For subscription information, call 1-800-627-9533 or visit www.americamagazine.org.

extended abstinence presents a serious challenge for many couples who practice NFP. Church documents assume that the abstinence required will be fairly short (seven to ten days per cycle) and fertile periods clearly identifiable. For many, this is simply not the case.

Many feel that NFP limits their lovemaking. Newlyweds whose wedding night or honeymoon falls in the fertile period and who need to avoid a pregnancy must abstain. Spouses whose work requires extensive travel may find that their time at home together does not match up with the infertile time, meaning that couples may regularly miss their window of opportunity to be together. Even couples without challenging work schedules will encounter times especially appropriate for lovemaking that do not fall within the infertile period. Some couples choose to ignore method rules and then become pregnant in times of hardship.

The postpartum period and breastfeeding also require a high degree of abstinence because of hormonal shifts. The transition to parenthood requires new parents to lean on each other and, ideally, is a time for them to grow closer as they face the new challenge of raising a family. Couples using NFP to space their children can find that precisely when they desire sexual intimacy to remain connected, it is frequently off limits. In time, the responsibilities of raising children may also chip away at couples' time for intimacy. Many begin to feel they must choose between feeding their marriage and the good of their family as a whole.

Couples share that other factors make it difficult to accurately chart signs of fertility. Stress, irregular sleep schedules, medications, medical conditions, and the transition into menopause make observing patterns in cervical mucus or temperature, both crucial to using NFP, less clear. Avoiding pregnancy in these situations means accepting extended abstinence, which for many is a damaging burden to their marriage.

Because physical affection is essential to both the partners' well-being and their bonding as a couple, spouses practicing NFP to avoid a pregnancy are encouraged to maintain high levels of physical affection while abstaining from intercourse. But even modest levels of physical affection can lead to arousal, and when that arousal cannot lead to intercourse, many experience frustration. The temptation to seek release in illicit ways increases. One woman shared, "As a married couple, we desperately wanted to be together, yet we felt we constantly had to be on guard with each other, just like when we were dating." Many couples scale back on physical affection to avoid temptation. Low levels of physical affection in a marriage leads to increased feelings of disconnection as a couple and to increased levels of stress, anxiety, and even depression.

The strain of prolonged abstinence causes many couples to engage in sexual activities outside of procreative intercourse, leading some to feel guilt and confusion, since these are considered immoral, yet bring much-needed closeness without the risk of pregnancy. Many couples report that the ban on these activities is the hardest part of Church teaching to follow and comprehend. One couple shared, "We felt that the teachings which prohibit nonprocreative sexual intimacy also were a burden, as we wanted to be united with one another and bring pleasure to one another; however, we instead had to sacrifice the unitive, as we were not able to take on the procreative." Another woman shared, "I feel trapped, not free about the rigidity of the rules of marital chastity. I feel that my sexuality, something that I thought was my gift to give to my husband, is limited."

Health problems also can complicate the use of NFP. Women with hormone abnormalities often experience complex cycles. While charting can help a woman identify health issues, many do not have access to health care professionals who are able to provide affordable solutions consonant with Catholic teaching. Second, NFP is especially stressful for couples who know that pregnancy would pose a grave health risk. For example, women who experience serious health conditions while pregnant must rely on NFP if they wish morally to avoid pregnancy. In extreme cases, a Catholic woman might use NFP to avoid pregnancy because another pregnancy could kill her. The only alternative offered by the Church is complete abstinence until menopause.

The financial burdens facing many families raise the stakes for couples practicing NFP. Many young people find themselves strapped with crippling student loan debt and unable to find decent work. "It seems that NFP is something that has far more serious consequences for those of us who are financially unstable," one woman wrote. "We make just enough to pay rent and buy groceries."

NFP promoters cite effectiveness rates comparable to artificial birth control, but many users are disappointed when, despite diligent adherence to method rules, they find themselves facing an unintended pregnancy. Couples who need to avoid pregnancy should be able to rely on their chosen method. Many feel deceived by the Church about the efficacy of NFP, and often experience a crisis of faith over whether to continue with natural family planning or go against Church teaching and rely on artificial birth control.

These couples want to be seen and heard by their bishops. Their hope remains that the bishops will consider that living out this teaching is often more stress inducing than life-giving. These issues demand not a mere reaffirmation of current teaching, but frank discussion and new pastoral solutions in keeping with Pope Francis's vision of a merciful Church.

CONSCIENCE AND CONTRACEPTION: TELLING OUR STORIES

My Mother's Burden

OLIVE BARNES

Humanae Vitae (*HV*) was published during my last year in a convent boarding school in Ireland. It was major news. The sister who taught us religious studies gave us each a copy and we spent many lessons studying and debating it. Our local bishop, Cahal Daly (later cardinal archbishop of Armagh) came to give a talk on it. My distinct memory of that talk was Bishop Daly equating all artificial contraceptives with murder. From our studies, we knew that barrier methods (condoms and caps) prevented the sperm from reaching the egg and the Pill prevented ovulation. I had some difficulty equating these with "murder." When I married seven years later, this was my strongest memory of the Church's teaching on artificial contraceptives. The credibility gap was a significant factor in my decision not to follow official Church teaching.

My fiancé and I discussed our plans for a family, I thought and prayed about them, and I discussed them with the priest who applied for our dispensation to marry (required as my fiancé was not Catholic). I re-read *Humanae Vitae* and I also read a series of articles on it from *The Tablet*. Advice on natural family planning was scant and, as my periods were not regular, it seemed this would be something of a lottery. Throughout all this, the clear message from priests and nuns whom I knew and respected was—inform your conscience and then, after prayer, decide. I went to see my doctor a few months before the wedding and was prescribed the contraceptive pill.

Humanae Vitae spoke of the unitive and procreative elements of sexual intercourse. My new husband and I needed to get to know each other. This was not just about sex. It was also about living together, sharing our daily lives, our hopes and fears, our finances. Our courtship had prepared us for some of this but the reality of any situation cannot be truly understood until you live it—we had not lived together before we were married though we had had sex a few times. We had to spend time establishing a truly stable relationship in which we could best raise children.

Some say that women's contraceptive decisions are motivated by career choices. I had a promising career. The opportunities open to me in 1975, even as a woman, were significant. This was not a motivation in deciding to postpone having children. We had both taken on a new role and we needed to adjust to that first. We both gave up some external activities so that we could spend that time together and build our relationship. In time I stopped taking the Pill and fell pregnant. My daughter was born two-and-a-half years after we married. Three more children followed, each spaced using barrier contraceptives. With four children, we agreed that our family was complete and a few years later I underwent a sterilization procedure. I had decided that, at nearly forty, if I were widowed and remarried I would not have more children, whereas in the same position my husband might wish to.

I was a full-time mother. The financial cost to us was significant. Our children did not have many of the consumer items that social pressure deemed essential to modern living; family holidays were self-catering camping; school trips and other extras had to be budgeted for. They did have a happy home life though (well, that at least is what they tell me!)

I compare my experience with that of my mother. Married exactly thirty years before me, she told me about the reality of her marriage, where the expectation was that she would keep producing baby after baby every year until she was worn out. She had five children and two miscarriages in the first seven years of her married life. I was the youngest child. After I was born, my parents stopped procreating. How? There were very few options at that time. The cost was an absolute absence of physical intimacy. I NEVER saw my parents cuddling or being in any way physically warm to each other. My mother and I agreed that that was a terrible burden for the male celibate leaders of the Church to lay on the shoulders of its followers. A devout and ardent Catholic whose watchword was "Trust in God," my mother was envious of the choice I had available to me.

CONSCIENCE AND CONTRACEPTION: TELLING OUR STORIES

Vatican Roulette

AMELIA BECK

Before marriage, I was advised by my general practitioner (GP) on the rhythm method. The resulting temperature chart, examined by the GP, did not give a clear result, but I was advised to avoid marital relations for the five days at the center of my monthly cycle.

Two months after marriage, and after faithfully following this advice, I became pregnant. Following the birth of this first child, we continued to follow the advice already given for regulating conception. This resulted in another birth fifteen months later, and a third birth nineteen months after that.

After this third birth in less than three years, my GP suggested using a barrier form of contraception. I discussed this with my husband but decided that it would be against my conscience. Having converted, I felt that I should not reject those teachings that I found "inconvenient."

I decided to restrict marital relations to the single day before menstruation was due. As my husband was a healthy, virile young man, this was an heroic sacrifice on his part. He always allowed any decision on contraceptive practice to be taken by me.

Ten months later, a fourth child was conceived. This was very alarming, as NFP obviously was not working. My GP then prescribed the Pill to regulate my (regular) menstruation.

After five months of agonies of conscience every time I took the Pill, I told my husband that I wanted to stop taking it. I suggested that marital relations be confined to a couple of days at the beginning of the monthly cycle. Surely this timing would work?

No, it did not. Two years later I gave birth for the fifth time. There were now just over six years between the first birth and the fifth birth. And a very unhappy husband, who told me on learning of this fifth pregnancy, "You CAN'T be pregnant!"

Following this last birth, I took the Pill for some months, suffering the same agonies of conscience. At this time I was pre-scribed antidepressants by my GP.

When this fifth baby was ten months old I had a severe nervous breakdown, precipitated by my decision, after confes-sion, that my husband and I could now only practice total abstinence. It took five years to recover from the breakdown I suffered, and it deeply—and adversely—affected family life.

Following this event, it was decided that sterilization was preferable. We had no further children.

The advent of such a large family, so early in our relation-ship, accompanied by the never-ending trauma of wondering every month if I was pregnant, did not contribute to a happy marriage. When practicing abstinence on such a scale, any affec-tion between us was, of necessity, vastly limited.

The agonies of conscience that I suffered were relieved only by the (at the time) lively hope that the Pill might be approved by the Church, thus providing Catholic couples with a reliable means to regulate their families, in accordance with the permission to so regulate granted by Vatican II. The dashing of this hope was a severe blow to me. "Vatican roulette" (still) rules!

CONSCIENCE AND CONTRACEPTION— TELLING OUR STORIES

Wanting a Different Life

GIOVANNA SOLARI-MASSON

My parents are strict Catholics and practiced NFP. My dad tells me he only wanted one child because he knew how much emotional and financial pressure comes from having multiple children; his grandmother died giving birth to her fourteenth child. My parents were happy in the beginning, but as well as having four children my mother suffered several miscarriages. One might say NFP didn't work for them, though my siblings and I were loved.

My story isn't uncommon for a working-class family from the 1970s. Dad worked six days a week to support us and instilled in us all the value of honest hard work. My mother was unhappy. She was simply not cut out to be a mother to so many children, she felt lonely with my dad working so much, and he had to work such long hours that he was too exhausted to attend to their relationship when he got home each day. Eventually the pressure was too much and my mother left us. As the oldest daughter I picked up the pieces. Oxford University didn't happen for me as planned and I ended up accepting a place at Kings' College London so that I could stay at home to help my dad look after my sisters and brother.

It is easy to say that you only need love to have children, but to fail to acknowledge the emotional and financial strain those children put on a relationship borders on negligence. I have two beautiful little girls aged six and seven, and a step-daughter aged thirteen. My husband and I are fully committed to helping them achieve everything they can and be everything they want to be. We both left jobs in the city to run our own business so that we can be with them when they get home from school.

Every day I read with my children, we supervise their homework, take them to various activities, involve them in cooking the family meal most nights, and we pray together every day. They have very different needs and as they are growing older their needs are becoming more pronounced. If I want them to be rounded individuals I need to have time, patience, and energy, and the more children I have the less time I will have for each of them.

I watched my parents suffer and I vowed that I would never have a life like theirs; I promised myself that it would be easier for my children. There was no way I was ever going to chance NFP. Educating and working myself into economic freedom was part of my journey and that meant controlling when and how many children I have, which has liberated me to grow into a person who can be a loving wife and mother. I couldn't let life just happen to me and suffer the consequences.

Before my children were born I used any number of artificial birth control methods. When my youngest was one year old my wonderful husband said, "You suffered chemicals to stop us having children until we were ready, it doesn't seem fair that you carry on." He had a vasectomy. God bless him.

CONSCIENCE AND CONTRACEPTION: TELLING OUR STORIES

A "Millennial's" Perspective

EMMA JANE HARRIS

I converted to Catholicism from an atheist background in my early twenties. Overcoming the psychological barrier to a meta-physical reality wrought by a heavily materialistic education was difficult. To further compound matters, my parents are liberal feminists who regard organized religion with contempt. I did not belong to a church community, I had no Catholic friends except for those I knew through university, and I had little understanding of day-to-day Catholic life.

I converted for many reasons, one of them being the gospel's subversive call to a radical love. When I converted, I was embraced by the Church. I was overwhelmed, but not surprised, by how welcoming I found its people to be. By that time I had experienced many of life's milestones—love, sex, loss, and bereavement—and I had long since decided not to get pregnant (yet). None of my close friends is married, none has children, and all of them use artificial contraception. This is standard among my peers—we so-called millennials. Our sexual relationships vary—some of my friends have casual sex, others don't. And while my generation recognizes the kind of relationships I have experienced—loving, committed, equal, unmarried—the

Church does not. I am not arguing that what is popular is necessarily right, but are we all in error?

Continuing my education and securing a job are necessary—an unstable home situation means that I have no fallback and financial matters have always been a concern. I do not want my fiancé to have to assume the stressful and limiting role of breadwinner, compromising his own career and life choices. Like him and others of my generation, I assume the opportunities we have for education, work, a loving relationship, and taking responsibility for our reproductive decisions to be our rights. Exercising these rights is a considered and well-meaning choice that I am thankful for. I do not think the God I believe in wishes to prevent me from being the best, most free, most openly loving person I can be. Motherhood, now, would prevent that.

Why have sex at all, then? I hold that sex is more than a functional tool and that being in love means wanting to be in it forever (though whether or not that pans out is another matter entirely). I do not wish to denigrate the mystery of marriage or of procreative sex, but rather to elevate the status of *all* love, and sexuality as an expression of that love and the hope it expresses.

I am uncomfortable whenever the Church discusses young people's relationships—especially recently, apropos the gay marriage debate—because I find that talk inevitably comes back to a question of functionality. Our relationships are authentic depending on *how they function*. I am in love. Is that a function? Does my love merely facilitate another, bodily purpose—that of procreation? Of course not—I know that in my very bones. And funnily enough, the way that I know this, and believe that my love is transcendent and mysterious, is the same way that I know and believe in God, too.

The primary status of love over procreation is proven by the fact that heterosexual couples can enter into the sacrament of marriage even if they cannot procreate (whether for medical reasons, or due to age, for example). However, if a man and woman marry without intending to love one another and live a

Catholic life, their marriage may not be regarded as valid. Similarly in the sacrament of the priesthood, celibacy is a primary element; a priest who admits an intention to having sex would not be a viable candidate. There is a distinction between the elements of a sacrament that are necessary and those that are contingent. Procreation must play handmaiden to the love that creates it.

I did not convert because of the Church's teachings on sexuality and gender but for Christianity's central truths and the Church's ability to safeguard them. It is always disappointing when the very truths it seeks to propagate so that people like myself can be converted are obfuscated by anxieties about sex. While the Church works out its complex and contradictory relationship with gender, sexuality, and the millennial generation, I have a life to live and work to do.

SAME-SEX MARRIAGE AND THE CATHOLIC COMMUNITY

MARGARET A. FARLEY

In the development of Catholic sexual ethics, certain concerns have been central. The primary moral rule has been "No sex outside of marriage." Sex is good, as early Christian writers insisted, since it is part of creation, but it is disordered as a result of original sin. Hence, sex as an inordinate and powerful drive must be constrained and channeled. Moreover, it needs to be justified by an intention to procreate, and essential to this is gender complementarity between men and women. These principles left no room for any positive valuation of homosexual relationships.

In the twentieth and twenty-first centuries, however, these foundations of sexual ethics began to be questioned. New biblical, theological, and historical studies of the roots of moral norms, new understandings of sexuality itself, and new shifts in economic and social life all contributed to major developments even in Catholic ethics. The dominant historical motifs underwent significant changes. The idea that the procreation of children is the sole justification for sexual activity is gone (a shift that is visible in the documents of Vatican II, in *Humanae Vitae* [*HV*], and in subsequent church teaching). The view of sexuality as fundamentally disordered has also gone from much Catholic

This is an edited version of an article that first appeared in *The Tablet* on September 25, 2014—published with permission of the publisher: http://www.thetablet.co.uk/.

thought. Although moral theologians still underline the potential of sex for sinfulness (as in sex abuse, rape, exploitation, adultery, and so forth), the almost total suspicion of its destructive power has been seriously modified. Rigid stereotypes of male/female complementarity have also been softened: gender equality, the mutuality of sexual relationships, an appreciation of shared possibilities and responsibilities now appear in Catholic as well as Protestant theologies of marriage and family.

However, the motifs of out-of-control sex, a procreative norm, and gender complementarity continue to appear in Catholic official (and some popular) assessments of same-sex activity. The procreative norm is relativized for heterosexual relations, but it returns when homosexual relations are at issue. The view of sex as disordered is gone for heterosexual sex, but it seems alive and well in judgments made about gay and lesbian sex. Rigid views of male/female complementarity are modified for general social roles, but fundamental gender difference suddenly reappears when critics take aim at an acceptance of same-sex relations.

But what *is* marriage that would seem to make it inappropriate for persons in same-sex partnerships? Many theologians who look for the core reality of marriage point to the consent of the partners in the form of a covenant or contract. In other words, marital commitment, mutually pledged, seems to be at the heart of the meaning of marriage. But "marital" commitment is a special form of commitment, a special form of covenant. It is a commitment to a permanent blending of loves, a weaving of a "fabric" of life together that embraces moments of powerful intensity but also the "everydayness" of life. It is a commitment to fruitfulness in love—fruitfulness that can take many forms. Finally, the marital commitment is a commitment to community and, if it is Christian, it is a commitment made individually and jointly to God.

Now what in this description of the core of marriage would not fit same-sex relationships that are marked by profound commitments to love, to be faithful to the uniqueness of their love, to be fruitful together in myriad ways through the gift of their love, and to anchor their love and life in community? Ah, for critics, there is still one stumbling block. They insist that there is one other element essential to the meaning of marriage: gender differentiation between spouses. Forms of marriage may change from era to era or from culture to culture; you might take away love; you might take away genuine choice; you might take away specific ceremonies; but there is one thing you cannot take away: marriage is always between a man and a woman.

But need this be so? Today the meanings of gender have become sufficiently problematized so that gender difference cannot simply be assumed as central to marriage in the same way as in the past. Karl Rahner's reflection on the sacrament of marriage considers it in terms of its symbolic relation to the love between Christ and the Church, as described by St. Paul: "Husbands, love your wives as Christ loves the Church; and wives, love your husbands as the Church loves Christ" (cf. Eph 5:29–33). Rahner says quite simply: the point here is not the gender assignment of roles—which is culturally conditioned; the point is the *unity* between spouses. Hence, we can just as well reverse role assignments: "Wives, love your husbands as Christ loves the Church; and husbands, love your wives as the Church loves Christ."[1]

For many, marriage is understood as between two equal persons. For each person, the gender of the other matters. But for the institution and sacrament of marriage, it need not matter. In a world where it would not matter whether persons were gay or straight, marriage would still be as important as it is today. Indeed, it might finally be as important as it should be.

The Scriptures tell us that God is present with us. We believe that particular human experiences are open to God's self-revelation in remarkable ways. We identify some of these ways as "sacraments." The Catholic sensibility discerns the presence of God around and in and among us. We may interpret the sacrament of marriage in the light of these beliefs, and sense that same-sex marriages, for those called to them, are or can be such experiences of the presence of God—manifest not only to the partners in marriage but to the Church and the world.

The marital sacrament is in the event of covenanting, of "marrying," but also in the life that continues from there. The grace of committed loves—shaped and grounded in faith—is not all at once. The story of commitments is importantly in their beginnings, yes, and in their end (lived out faithfully unto their consummation or fulfillment), but it is the "between" that counts most. Hence, the sacrament of marriage (presence and sign) is in the everyday, in the choices to ratify commitments, the efforts to grow in simple patience, kindness, understanding, and forgiveness, and the "little by little" of welcoming love. All of this can be true of same-sex marriage.

Marriage as a framework of life and love is both a means and an end. Its ultimate telos reaches into the mystery of God, into radical communion with God and with all other persons in God. This is how grace works: not only in peak moments of covenant, but in strategies for compassionate respect, enduring fidelity, hope in an unlimited future, and step-by-step courageous, faith-formed love.

The Catholic community can understand all of this, and help it to come to be.

NOTES

1. Karl Rahner, "Marriage as a Sacrament," *Theological Investigations*, vol. 10, trans. David Bourke (New York: Herder and Herder, 1973), 218–21.

SAME-SEX LOVE: TELLING OUR STORIES

Living under the Radar, or Celebrating Family in All Its Forms?

Sophie Stanes and Deborah Woodman

In 2009, at our civil partnership reception, surrounded by more than 120 family and friends, we toasted to "Family: in all its forms." Little did we know the highs and lows we would experience over the next six years in our living out of "being family."

For many women and girls their first experience of discrimination in the Church is based on their gender. When it is layered over with sexuality that is "other," one experiences double discrimination. In England it is possible for two women to exist in the Church under this particular "cloak of invisibility." It is not unusual for two women to attend Mass together, to be readers or eucharistic ministers, to volunteer or lead parish events. Our gifts (both practical and financial) are welcomed—depended upon even—as long as we are quiet about our "true" identity. But when we approach the institution we belong to for official validation and pastoral support, it is with trepidation.

When we, as two women, chose to be lifelong partners our focus was on strengthening that bond, living in love, growing in mutual support to each other, and sharing our gifts and talents with our community, Church, and world. We are drawn to the concept of the domestic church. It means that the detail of our everyday lives, our commitment to working for a better world, our hospitality to friend and stranger has the possibility of being grace filled. This choice puts us on an equal footing with other Catholic families, rather than wrangling over who is worthy of the label *married.*

The primary focus of our relationship has not been on procreation, although through access to fertility treatment that is now possible. Sometimes we have seen heterosexual couples get married with the express intention of having children. When Mother Nature does not cooperate, the relationship can be placed under significant strain, whereas for us, children would still be a gift—not an expectation or entitlement.

Being different from the norm means that each sacrament or pastoral situation has to be navigated afresh: taking from Church teaching what is life-giving; making relevant what can be helpful; filtering out the dubious—just as many of us women have learned to do with exclusive language. It has also been our experience that most practicing Catholic women who identify as gay, lesbian, or bisexual take their faith seriously (and with an essential dose of humor). We have had to weigh up how to reconcile two foundational aspects of our identity: faith and sexuality. It is a privileged position: to witness to one's faith in the LGBT community and to witness to one's sexual identity in the Catholic Church.

We have seen the Church at its best and its worst. We had a wonderful thanksgiving Mass in a community center on the occasion of our civil partnership but we were refused the use of every church we approached. Each time a different reason was given, even when we were at pains to point out that this was not a pseudomarriage ceremony or mockery of the sacrament.

Part of our reason for entering into a legal partnership was to ensure that if either of us had a biological child, the other partner was automatically considered to be a legal parent. This stability was important to both of us, and our concept of family. After securing a small amount of initial funding from our local health authority, we embarked on a long journey of assisted conception, covering IUI, IVF, known donor insemination, and embryo adoption.

We were fortunate to become pregnant with twins through IVF in 2012, only to suffer the heartbreak of losing them at twenty-five and a half weeks. Again we saw the Church at its best and its worst. A priest friend jumped on his motorbike late at night to come to the hospital and baptize T and G in their precious few moments of life. He accompanied us in those dark hours and three weeks later buried them in a beautiful funeral liturgy that we compiled together. Our home church dedicated Mass to us without us even needing to ask. We felt carried and supported by friends and family at a time when we could not carry ourselves. God's grace was truly at work. In contrast, the official Roman Catholic hospital chaplain denied us holy communion the day after our loss simply for being a same sex couple.

It is this contrast between official teaching and unofficial practice that is so damaging. As long as the power to control access to sacraments on a personal interpretation or whim exists, it leaves us as second-class citizens who give all we can but risk everything when we ask.

SAME-SEX LOVE: TELLING OUR STORIES

"The Glory of God Is a Human Being Fully Alive"

URSULA HALLIGAN

> *Our lives begin to end the day we become silent about things that matter.*
>
> **—Martin Luther King**

I was a good Catholic girl, growing up in 1970s Ireland where homosexuality was an evil perversion. It was never openly talked about but I knew it was the worst thing on the face of the earth. So when I fell in love with a girl in my class in school, I was terrified. Rummaging around in the attic a few weeks ago, an old diary brought me right back to December 20th, 1977. "These past few months must have been the darkest and gloomiest I have ever experienced in my entire life," my seventeen-year-old self wrote. The diary goes on,

> There have been times when I have even thought about death, of escaping from this world, of sleeping untouched by no-one forever. I have been so depressed, so sad and so confused. There seems to be no one I can turn to, not even God. I've poured out

This is an edited version of an article that first appeared in *The Irish Times*, Thursday, June 4, 2015—reprinted with permission.

my emotions, my innermost thoughts to him and get no relief or so-called spiritual grace. At times I feel I am talking to nothing, that no God exists. I've never felt like this before, so empty, so meaningless, so utterly, utterly miserable.

Because of my upbringing, I was revolted at the thought that I was in love with a member of my own sex. This contradiction nearly drove me crazy. These two strands of thought jostled within me, pulling me in opposite directions.

I loved a girl and I knew that wasn't right; my mind was constantly plagued with the fear that I was a lesbian. I hated myself. I felt useless and worthless and very small and stupid. I had one option, and only one option. I would be "normal," and that meant locking myself in the closet and throwing away the key.

Over the years I watched each of my siblings date, party, get engaged, get married, and take for granted all the joys and privileges of their state-acknowledged relationship, and never once did I openly express my feelings. I buried myself in books or work. I was careful how I talked and behaved. I never knew what it was like to live spontaneously, to go with the flow, to trust my instincts. Emotionally, I have been in a prison since the age of seventeen—a prison where I lived a half-life, repressing an essential part of my humanity, the expression of my deepest self, my instinct to love. It's a part of themselves that heterosexual people take for granted, like breathing air. The world is tailor-made for them. At every turn society assumes and confirms heterosexuality as the norm. This culminates in marriage when the happy couple is showered with an outpouring of overwhelming social approval.

For me, there was no first kiss, no engagement party, no wedding, and up until a short time ago, no hope of any of these things. Now, at the age of fifty-four, in a (hopefully) different Ireland, I wish I had broken out of my prison cell a long time ago. I feel a sense of loss and sadness for precious time spent wasted in fear and isolation.

Homophobia was so deeply embedded in my soul, I resisted facing the truth about myself, preferring to live in the safety of my prison. In the privacy of my head, I had become a roaring, self-loathing homophobe, resigned to going to my grave with my shameful secret. And I might well have done that if the referendum hadn't come along.

Now, I can't quite believe the pace of change that's sweeping across the globe in support of gay marriage. I never thought I'd see the day that a government minister would come out as gay and encounter almost nothing but praise for his bravery. I began to realize that possibilities existed that I'd never believed would ever exist.

I told a friend and the world didn't end. I told my mother, and the world didn't end. Then I realized that I could leave the prison completely or stay in the social equivalent of an open prison. The second option would mean telling a handful of people but essentially going on as before, silently colluding with the prejudices that still find expression in casual social moments. It's the easier of the two options, particularly for those close to me. Those who love you can cope with you coming out, but they're wary of you "making an issue" of it.

The game changer was the marriage equality referendum. It pointed me toward the first option: telling the truth to anyone who cares. Twenty or thirty years ago, it would have taken more courage than I had to tell the truth. Today, it's still difficult but it can be done with hope—hope that most people in modern Ireland embrace diversity and would understand that I'm trying to be helpful to other gay people leading small, frightened, incomplete lives. If my story helps even one seventeen-year-old schoolgirl, struggling with her sexuality, it will have been worth it.

As a person of faith and a Catholic, I believe a yes vote is the most Christian thing to do. I believe the glory of God is the human being fully alive and that this includes people who are gay.

SAME-SEX LOVE: TELLING OUR STORIES

Getting Hooked: Being Lesbian and Becoming Catholic

EVE TUSHNET

When I became Catholic in 1998, as a college sophomore, I didn't know any other gay Christians. I'd been raised in a kind of pointillist Reform Judaism, almost entirely protected from homophobia; when I realized I was gay it was, if anything, a relief. I thought I finally had an explanation for the persistent sense of difference I'd felt since early childhood. This sheltered upbringing may help explain my sunny undergraduate confidence that even though I knew of literally nobody else who had ever tried to be both unashamedly gay and obediently Catholic, I was totally going to do it. No problem, guys, I got this.

Things look different now. I hope I've learned a few things about the dangers of sophomoric self-confidence. There are times when my relationship with the Catholic Church feels a lot like Margaret Atwood's ferocious little poem:

You fit into me
like a hook into an eye

This is an edited extract from an article that first appeared in *The Atlantic* on May 30, 2013—published with permission of the publisher: http://www.theatlantic.com /world/.

a fish hook
an open eye

Many Christian churches are beginning to integrate gay marriage into their theology. Their preexisting theology—not only on marriage but on creation, embodiment, and scriptural interpretation—has begun to shift to match the new unisex or gender-neutral model of marriage. With so many more options for gay Christians, why stick with the fishhook? Here is an attempt at my own answer.

The biggest reason I don't just de-pope myself is that I fell in love with the Catholic Church. Very few people just "believe in God" in an abstract way; we convert, or stay Christian, within a particular church and tradition. I didn't switch from atheistic post-Judaism to "belief in God," but to Catholicism: the incarnation and the crucifixion, Michelangelo and Wilde, St. Francis and Dorothy Day. I loved the Church's beauty and sensual glamor. I loved her insistence that seemingly irreconcilable needs could both be met in God's overwhelming love: justice and mercy, reason and mystery, a Savior who is fully God and also fully human. I even loved her tabloid, gutter-punching side, the way Catholics tend to mix ourselves up in politics and art and pop culture. (I love that side a little less now, but it's necessary.)

I didn't expect to understand every element of the faith. It is a lot bigger than I am. I'm sure there are psychological reasons for my desire to find a God and a Church I could trust entirely: I don't think I have a particularly steady moral compass, for example. I'm better at falling in love than finding my way, more attuned to eros than to ethics. Faith is no escape from the need for personal moral judgment; the Church is meant to form your conscience, not supersede it. There are many things that, if the Catholic Church commanded them, I think would have prevented me from becoming Catholic. But I do think it was okay to enter the Church without being able to justify all of her teachings on my own.

At the time of my baptism the Church's teaching on homosexuality was one of the ones I understood the least. I didn't understand the teaching, but had agreed to accept it as the cost of being Catholic. To receive the Eucharist I had to sign on the dotted line (they make you say, "I believe all that the Catholic Church believes and teaches" when they bring you into the fold), and I longed intensely for the Eucharist, so I figured, everybody has to sacrifice something. God doesn't promise that he'll only ask you for the sacrifices you agree with and understand.

At the moment I do think I understand the Church's teaching better than I did then—but check back with me in a few years. But this doesn't mean that I think the Catholic Church is perfect when it comes to gay people. I spend a lot of time these days working with people who are trying to make the Church a home for gay people. It's painfully far from that now. A friend of mine wrote about the role played by Jewish converts to Catholicism in improving the Church's relationship to Judaism. The gay, celibate Christians I know feel a similar responsibility toward our churches.

The Church needs to grow and change in response to societal changes. We can do so much better in serving the needs of gay/queer/same-sex-attracted Catholics, especially the next generation. But I think gay Catholics can also offer a necessary witness to the broader society. By leading lives of fruitful, creative love, we can offer proof that sexual restraint isn't a death sentence (or an especially boring form of masochism). Celibacy can offer some of us radical freedom to serve others.

If I believed that Catholicism condemned gay people to a barren, loveless life, I would not be Catholic, full stop. All people have a call from God to give and receive love. For me the call to love takes the form of service to those in need, prayer, and, above all, loving friendship. Friendship was once a form of Christian kinship—see Alan Bray's beautiful historical study, *The Friend*.[1] It was honored by society, guided by theology, beautified by liturgy. It was a form of love experienced and highly praised by Jesus himself.

Renewing this Christian understanding of friendship would help to make the Church a place where gay people have more opportunities for devoted, honored love than in the secular world—not fewer. Many of us—including single straight people, and married people of every orientation—long for deeper and more lasting friendships. The cultural changes that would better nourish celibate gay Christians, then, would be good for everyone else as well.

NOTE

1. Alan Bray, *The Friend* (Chicago: University of Chicago Press, 2006).

BEING GOOD
AND DOING BAD?

Virtue Ethics and
Sexual Orientation

KATIE GRIMES

While condemning homosexual orientation as "objectively dis-ordered" since it tends toward "homosexual acts" that are "intrinsically evil," the magisterium nonetheless cautions that this orientation "cannot be considered sinful" because it often "is experienced as a given, not as something freely chosen."[1] Seeking to live within the limits of Church teaching, a growing number of Catholics declare themselves openly gay but res-olutely celibate. The lesbian Catholic blogger Eve Tushnet describes "accepting sexuality" as

> being honest about…where your sexual desires are being directed, and not feeling that this area of your life is somehow shut off from God or turned away from God in a way that the rest of your life isn't. It means not separating out your sexuality and your sexual orientation by saying they need to be repressed or destroyed in some way.[2]

However, if the magisterium speaks the truth when it clas-sifies sexual relationships between people of the same sex as unconditionally evil, then homosexual women and men should seek to eradicate their orientation toward what the magisterium classifies as the categorical evil of gay sex. To make this argument, I turn to Thomistic virtue theory. It helps to explain why, if gay sex is evil, then so is the desire for gay sex. And if the desire for gay sex is evil, then so is it evil to make the desire for gay sex a constitutive part of one's personality.

Virtue theory describes the relationship between actions, habits, and character. We become what we do and we do what we are. Good people do good things just as people become good by doing good. The best way to do good deeds is to build good habits. According to Thomas Aquinas, our thoughts and internal desires also qualify as morally consequential. While a person surely can do the right thing even when she does not want to, she is much more likely to act rightly when she derives pleasure from goodness.

Virtue theory cares not just about what we do but also who we are. It therefore recognizes that our thoughts and desires possess more than merely instrumental importance. Rightly ordered thoughts and desires are good in and of themselves. A good person does not merely do the right thing; she both desires to do the right thing and takes pleasure in acting rightly.

This allows us to identify moral goodness as a hierarchy that encompasses the entire human person. A person who does the right thing but does not derive pleasure from it is just not as good as a person who does the right thing and enjoys doing so. Conversely, a person who refrains from committing evil but derives deep pleasure at the thought of inflicting evil also falls short of virtue. Of course, the one who commits evil and loves it ranks lowest.

Here theory conforms to common sense notions of goodness. For example, while we surely believe it better for persons to refrain from indulging their appetite for inflicting pain and suffering on animals, we would still consider it quite immoral and disturbing that a person would derive pleasure from thinking about the suffering of sentient beings. We would want a person who derives pleasure from the thought of torturing animals to purge herself of these desires. We certainly would not want that person to "accept" her affinity for torture as a constituent part of her personality.

When people contend that we ought to condemn sexual relationships between people of the same sex as unconditionally evil while accepting gayness as a sinless identity, they act like one who calls the torture of animals categorically evil but proclaims the desire to torture animals morally good. As virtue theory reminds us, it is evil to find evil pleasurable or desirable. For this reason, if so-called homosexual acts qualify as evil, then so does deriving pleasure from thought of them.

If the magisterium speaks the truth about so-called homosexual acts, then even celibate lesbians form their identity around a desire and affinity for evil. What else is sexual attraction except a desire to experience sexual closeness with another person? Strip away everything related to the desire for sexual relationship with another woman and "lesbian" dissolves as a coherent identity. A lesbian, by definition, possesses a constitutive and predominant sexual attraction to other women and not men. Magisterial teaching perceives homosexual persons as uniquely incapable of cultivating sexual virtue.

Tushnet rightly echoes Pope Francis's call for the Church to make room for its lesbian and gay members, but perhaps lesbian and gay Catholics struggle to find a home within ordinary Catholic parishes because there is no place for them in the pages of magisterial teaching. The magisterium tells homosexual persons they can be but they must not do. But, if one should not do, then neither should one be. Gayness cannot be good as a sexual identity but bad as a sexual activity. Virtue just does not work that way.

NOTES

1. Letter to the Bishops of the Catholic Church on the Pastoral Care of Homosexual Persons, par. 3; USCCB, "Always Our Children: A Pastoral Message to the Parents of Homosexual Children and Suggestions for Pastoral Ministers."

2. Sean Salai, SJ, "'Gay and Catholic': An Interview with Author Eve Tushnet," *America*, July 3, 2014, at http://americamag azine.org/content/all-things/gay-and-catholic-interview-author-eve-tushnet.

"WHAT'S LOVE GOT TO DO WITH IT?"

Women's Experience of Celibacy

JANETTE GRAY

Women's experience and understanding of their life commitment through the vow of celibacy has received very little attention over the centuries, though there have always been more female than male exponents of celibacy in Western Christianity. Most discourse about celibacy has been preoccupied with transgressions of the vow or with psychological problems arising from immature social and sexual development in its practitioners. In what follows I argue that, despite its apparent rejection of sexual pairing, women's celibacy can be understood as an expression of human sexuality.

The recurrence of celibacy across many varied societies and religious traditions suggests that it is as natural among humans as pair bonding in marriage and other partnerships. The Christian understanding of celibacy means a life totally dedicated to union with God through nonmarriage and sexual abstinence. This demands a valuing of sexuality and human relationships as integral to God's creation of humanity, but it also serves as an expression of the diversity of human relations, beyond the genital sexual.

To understand sexual renunciation in terms of denial of the body and sexuality restricts the humanity of the celibate person by promoting a dissociated view of reality. It confuses personal detachment with a selfish lack of responsible commitment to another. Such a negative understanding of celibacy has also been blamed for not containing or converting sexual needs in destructive personalities, and the sexual abuse of minors has been one dreadful consequence of this.[1]

Women's experience of celibacy calls for a better understanding of human sexual embodiment rooted in a positive Christian anthropology. This would acknowledge the different needs and expressions of celibate women's sexuality, rather than denying them. Theologies of the body that have addressed celibacy are concerned with how abstinence from sexual activity can be understood not to devalue sex, the body, or women's sexuality, but to represent wider human experiences of sexuality and relationships than sexual intercourse. A woman's celibacy that neither rejects the sexual nor relational in humanity is an expression of the search for union with God, mediated in the diversity of human relationships other than sexual partnership. A Christian theology of celibacy can show how God is love, even in situations where love appears unrequited, by manifesting a form of human love that does not depend on the reciprocity of a partner. In this way, celibacy illuminates the diversity that is human love in the many ways in which it manifests God's love.

Women with a creative attitude toward celibacy seek to unite the bodily and spiritual in loving service of God. This is an affirmation of the embodiment that is vital to the incarnational nature of Christian faith. Women celibates who have sought to understand their vocation in these terms report that the meaning of their lives is deepened through their appreciation of their sexuality and their bodies and not despite them.[2] They welcome the constant challenge of their sexuality and are vigilant about any tendency to body denial. Women celibates embody alternatives for other women who have been categorized only as a sex partner or heir producer. They give voice to all the different social and familial roles of women, including sisters, grandmothers, aunts, cousins, nannies, and the variety of women's friendships. Recent studies suggest that, when women's experience of an embodied, celibate sexuality is not based in abjection or denial of the body, it can challenge the negative concept of woman as sensual temptress that has informed past theologies of celibacy.[3]

Who is the God who is revealed through this celibate witness? Given that the God of creation is seen to bless sexual procreation and the depth of relationship represented by marriage, how does this square with celibacy?

Celibacy is a human experiment in God's love. It expresses a trust that the unchosen condition of many humans who love but receive little or no return of their love is not without meaning in terms of the whole of creation. Women's celibacy does not disregard this human need for love, but it does not idolize the satisfaction of this need. Rather, it is only possible within the hope of the reality of God's love. God's love is understood more in what is inexpressible in even the most satisfactory sexual love and through the absences that punctuate all human relating. To compromise such experience through any fantasized coupling with God or other sublimations of human relationship would deny the source of all love. The incarnational nature of women's celibacy reveals that God is found in the diversity of creation and human encounters, not in narcissism nor exclusively in the isolation of the couple.[4] Women's celibate experience that resists the denial of sexuality finds that God is love abiding in our human sexuality: God is love and is all our desire for love and to love. This celibacy embodies the knowledge that union with God and union with all whom we love are not unrealistic ideals but are partly realized in our present loving. They anticipate the fullness of loving union promised in the reign of God, no matter how deficient and pain filled our experiences of love in the present. Such an experience of women's celibacy that is open to sexuality proclaims the loving Creator's delight in variety while celebrating the saving God's overcoming of our limitations and enlivening the Spirit's communal transformation of aloneness.

NOTES

1. Cf. A. W. Richard Sipe, *Celibacy: A Way of Loving, Living and Serving* (Dublin: J Gill & Macmillan, 1996).

2. See Janette Gray, *Neither Exploiting nor Escaping Sex: Women's Experience of Celibacy* (Maynooth: St. Paul Publications, 1995).

3. Cf. William Loader, *Sexuality and the Jesus Tradition* (Grand Rapids: Eerdmans Publishing Co., 2005).

4. Cf. Lisa Isherwood, *The Power of Erotic Celibacy: Queering Heteropatriarchy* (New York: T&T Clark International, 2006).

SINGLED OUT

The Vocation to Solitude

PATRICIA STOAT

Being single isn't an unfortunate accident, something that you have to put a brave face on between attachments. Being single can be a vocation, an art form, a lifestyle, a way. It's different from marriage, and from the religious life. It is not, whatever may be said to the contrary, a lesser life than these, or a life less challenging or less complete.

"Single" in modern terminology is often used to mean "temporarily without a significant other." You may be a single parent, sharing your life with children. Many single people, women especially, are carers, with a dependent older relative to look after. When the person to whose care they have been devoted dies, they find themselves alone. There are those of us who simply never meet the right person; and those for whom perhaps there isn't a right person, whose vocation really is "to be different."

Discovering the single life as vocation can be painful. You expect to marry and have children; gradually you realize that this is not going to happen. This time in your life may be very confusing, as you hunt for the right path, run backward and forward, try this way and that, are never quite where you need to be, never in balance. For many single women, this can be a dark time.

You may find, and must get used to being, the odd one out. Humankind assumes the family, and single people don't quite fit into family life. You are free: but the price of your freedom may be loneliness. Solitude for some of us is a gift to be prized, for others solitude may be a burden to be endured.

The New Testament has little to say about family life, and what little it says is pretty straightforward: be kind to one another, care for one another, be faithful, fulfill your responsibilities, set a good example, and if you are a widow, don't gossip and don't drink too much.

Jesus' family are those "who hear the word of God and obey it" (Luke 11:28). This new family is woven of friends, disciples, all those who journey with Jesus. Women in this community are neither silent nor subordinate; and they do not appear to be dependents of men. They provide for the mission, offer hospitality, act as emissaries, lead communities, run businesses, and are counted among the prophets, apostles, martyrs, saints.

The Church celebrates Mary as mother, but also as Virgin. Virginity symbolizes freedom, the woman not constrained by custom or convention. Virginity was prized in the early Christian communities because virgins, women and men, were free of the encumbrances of family and society. The virgin was outside the bounds of law and custom, free to live for God alone. In the Christian worldview, the free woman has a place of honor.

This development reflects the new reality, the Church. In the Christian understanding, the outsider is the insider: the blind see, the dumb speak, and last are first. The creative heart is found not at the center, but among the poor and disregarded, on the periphery. This is where the outsiders, the single women, belong. On the margins, a bent woman stands upright and sings, "Alleluia," (Luke 13:10–13) Julian the Anchoress writes in English about her insights into the love of God, and Dorothy Day launches the *Catholic Worker*. They are all women outside the conventions and norms of their social contexts.

In the Church, and through participation in the life of the Church, I may come to see my singleness not as a lack or loss but as a blessing. The gospel offers me a new place to stand and take my bearings: from here, new horizons open, and being single becomes not a failure but an opportunity, a gift.

The spiritual traditions of the Christian faith are deep and rich. Acknowledging my single state as a gift, I have time, and I have space, to study, make retreats, walk as a pilgrim to holy places, engage with the art and music of the Christian centuries, and discover a certain confidence in the foolishness of God.

I come to value friendship, and learn to pay attention to the small things, flowers, and clouds, and a glass of wine at evening. I value holy hours, and vigils, and silence. I campaign for justice, and work for peace.

It's a privilege to be single, to be able to go where one pleases and follow the paths less trodden, to make discoveries and explore unknown territory and to pioneer new routes, take risks, seek buried treasure. It is a gift to be cherished, and in Christ, a blessing.

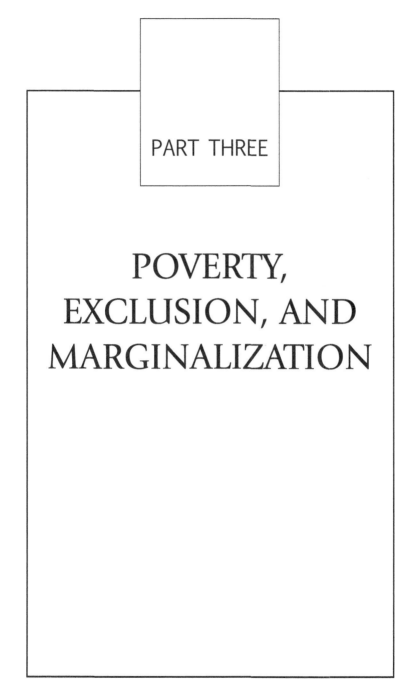

PART THREE

POVERTY, EXCLUSION, AND MARGINALIZATION

INTRODUCTION
TO PART THREE

Globalization has ushered in a complex era of new demands for labor and resources that impact on families in many ways, both as opportunities for change and threats to stable social systems. Globalized markets have not only enabled the expansion of the middle classes in many countries but they have also increased inequalities between the richest and the poorest people. Harsh new environments have been created in which women are often in the frontline of the struggle to defend themselves and their children against new forms of economic, sexual, and social exploitation. The more pluralist, transient, and cosmopolitan societies that are developing in many parts of the world in response to globalization present many challenges to the Church, including the increasing number of interfaith marriages and the significant growth of single parent families—often led by women.

The essays in this section explore some of these issues, once again demonstrating that local Catholic communities can be rich sources of solidarity and support among women as they seek to express their faith in Christ, sometimes in extreme conditions of poverty and suffering. All of the essays in this section describe families that are far from the idealized model of the nuclear family found in official church teaching, yet each of them, in their very diversity, their struggles and their bonds of connection and love, points the way toward a more inclusive and pastorally responsive and responsible approach to families.

Ana Lourdes Suárez and Gabriela Zengarini offer a moving insight into the lives of three women in a poor neighborhood in Buenos Aires. Each of these women has endured

133

unthinkable suffering in the context of family life and mother-hood. They have drawn upon their experiences of violence, poverty, and loss and their hope in Christ to help others, "form-ing families of God where every son and daughter is equal, and where leadership takes the form of accompanying."

As a Catholic woman married to a Hindu man, Astrid Lobo Gajiwala describes the situations she encounters among women in India in the context of both poverty and interfaith families. She points out how many of the assumptions in the *Lineamenta* distributed in preparation for the 2014 Synod on the Family had no bearing on the lives of poor, illiterate women for whom marriage is often "a prison sentence, replete with marital rape, domestic violence, isolation, subservience to the point of slavery, and unplanned pregnancies that have fatal consequences for both mother and child." Alongside these challenges of extreme poverty and violence, the Church must also formulate an effective pastoral response to those in inter-faith families, in a subcontinent where Catholics constitute less than 2 percent of the population. Lobo Gajiwala appeals for a more inclusive appreciation of the riches that Catholic women in interfaith marriages bring to the Church, offering models of dialogue and understanding that emerge from "their daily encounter of the unfathomable mystery and immensity of God as revealed in another religion."

Nontando Hadebe also identifies problems with the model of the nuclear family in the 2014 *Lineamenta*, drawing on her pastoral and theological work with African families. Like Anne Arabome in part 1, she appeals for a contextualized African theology that might produce "more liberating interpre-tations" of Church teaching. Focusing particularly on the prob-lem of maternal mortality in sub-Saharan Africa, she argues for a more positive approach to reproductive rights, informed by "the voices and experiences of those who are affected by mater-nal death—namely, the world's poorest women and their fam-ily communities."

Agnes Brazal discusses the challenge posed to Filipino families by the migration of women to seek work abroad, in the context of growing economic pressures produced by globalization. She argues that the migration of mothers has been shown to have a more profound impact on children than the migration of fathers, not least because fathers are seldom prepared to take over the work of raising children and managing households. Brazal shows how church teachings on family life have adapted to new situations over the last century, and she appeals for a further adaptation that would encourage men as well as women to develop "the capacity for the other" that is entailed in raising children and managing a household.

The essays in this section suggest that, if Pope Francis's vision of a poor Church of the poor is to become a reality, then it is essential to recognize the many ways in which poverty has a particular impact on women. Such recognition requires setting aside doctrinal absolutes in order to engage with the realities of women's lives. That means listening to and learning from poor women's stories of faith in the context of their experiences of violence, marginalization, and domestic and social breakdown.

"A MYSTICISM OF OPEN EYES"

Catholic Women's Voices from a Marginal Neighborhood of Buenos Aires

ANA LOURDES SUÁREZ AND GABRIELA ZENGARINI
(TRANS. SÉVERINE DENEULIN)

> *This is where we are making the Kingdom, it is not*
> *to wait... but it is here and now in the reality that*
> *we find God and where we are learning to love.*
> *Prayer is not prayer if it is not with the face of Christ*
> *here in the brother and in the sister.*
> **—Irish nun who lived in Cuartel V**

Cuartel V is a neighborhood of about fifty thousand residents in the northwest outskirts of Buenos Aires. It is one of the poorest, most segregated and isolated neighborhoods. Three resident Catholic women relate the stories of their families and their journeys of reconciliation and transformation, which led them, in turn, to reconcile and transform the neighborhood.

Vicky was born in 1958, the eldest of three. Her father was

This is an extract from a paper originally published as "Gracias a que caminamos con ellas: Prácticas de mujeres en barrios marginales desde una mística de ojos abiertos," in *Ciudad Vivida. Prácticas de Espiritualidad en Buenos Aires*, coord. Virginia Azcuy (Buenos Aires: Editorial Guadalupe, Buenos, 2014), 73–115—published with permission.

prone to alcoholism and gambling. The family migrated to the city in search of a better life. As a child, Vicky had to defend her mother and brothers from her father's violence. Her brother was left disabled due to domestic violence, and her mother died from depression when Vicky was an adolescent. Vicky has been working since she was a child, but still managed to finish secondary school. She started university, but had to abandon her schooling because she became pregnant, and because of poor public transportation. She is now teaching in a school for adults in the neighborhood. She is a member of the parish council, and has eight children from two relationships.

Delia was born around 1957 in a rural area in the north, and is the fourth of ten children. When her mother and elder sisters moved to Buenos Aires to work in domestic service, the youngest child was six months old. In her childhood, she endured domestic burdens, her mother's migration, and the figure of a father she had to "look after." She left school at the age of ten to look after her siblings and her father. She was brought up to be submissive: "The woman does not have voice." She migrated to Buenos Aires at fourteen to work as a domestic worker and had no legal documentation until she was eighteen. She has one daughter, has completed secondary school and catechist formation, and is now parish secretary. Her life has been marked by cancer believed to be terminal, from which she has since recovered. Her husband died young. She works in a women's health center founded by nuns.

Marta was born in 1963 in the province of Buenos Aires, the youngest of nine children. Her mother died when she was nine. As a child, she suffered work, neglect, violence, and exclusion. She never went to school, and defines herself as illiterate. She often went hungry and was undernourished, because of which she became anemic. Her father, a drunkard, was very violent with the children: "We have many scars," she says. She has worked in domestic service and waste collection, has nine children, and never legally married. Her common-law husband spent eleven years in jail, and she is in charge of four additional children abandoned by his previous partner. Three of her children are drug addicts and one committed suicide, which affected her terribly. She is now the coordinator of the parish soup kitchen, and a huge life-giving presence. In her kitchen she receives young people at risk of drug addiction and organizes special activities for them. She is the pillar of the community formed around the soup kitchen.

It is through their insertion in relationships soaked in what Johann Baptist Metz calls a "mysticism of open eyes" that Vicky, Delia, and Marta were able to break the circle of exclusion and become bearers of the gospel. This mysticism of open eyes is incarnated in the practices of mutual listening, accompaniment, service, and social commitment.

The three women grew up in deeply adverse circumstances: poverty, domestic burdens, child labor, and death of or abandonment by their mothers. They all suffered physical or symbolic violence from their fathers. Being listened to helped them to heal, and listening gave life to others:

> I like it, and it did me a lot of good because I got out all the things from when I was a child....Today I tell this as a story...because I have processed it...but before, each time I tried to talk about it...I cried and cried and cried: Why did this happen to me?...And with time the wounds healed, and in fact, I now facilitate this mutual listening for other women....I am helping other women so that they can live. [Delia]

> And yes, I have learned a lot from my father... because I believe that one of the biggest graces I have is having learned to forgive. This is why I have been able to forgive my father, a lot of things I was able to forgive him....And when one is able to forgive, one starts to understand and see the person from another place, and I could understand why my father was the way he was. [Vicky]

This healing process extends to the whole community. Vicky coordinates a series of educational, productive, and cultural activities in the neighborhood. Delia manages a mutual listening group, and Marta the soup kitchen. From these places, these women weave together various communities, which become in turn spaces of healing and reconciliation. They are forming families of God where every son and daughter is equal, and where leadership takes the form of accompanying:

> We were organizing these activities with the nuns, equally with the priest....Then we were one, there was no difference in the church, in the organization, in the neighbors: we are all....From the catechesis new leaders are formed, and we are the ones leading today these processes...but I never do anything alone, I never put myself as the single leader, I prefer they don't know that I am the stamp on the work. [Vicky]

> There are many children who come and eat, many mothers, many elderly people, and thanks to the strength of Marta, we keep going, in health or without health, in rain or no rain, Marta does not make black and white distinctions, she receives us like we are....I was in crisis and she opened the door, and thanks to her I am better. [person speaking of Marta]

To accept history and transform it is part of following Jesus and being faithful to his Spirit. We believe that the gospel was reenacted in Cuartel V, through the work of the Holy Spirit, in the actions and words of these women of faith, a faith that God is present even in the harshest realities and most painful moments of life, and in the communities to which these women gave birth, and to which they continue to give life.

CHALLENGING FAMILIES

Indian Women Speak
from the Margins

ASTRID LOBO GAJIWALA

The Synods on the Family in 2014 and 2015 have generated a great deal of interest. The people in the pews—determined to get their voices heard—have held consultations, gathered in group discussions, answered online questionnaires, written open letters to the pope, and posted messages on social media.

The majority of my Indian sisters, however, remain outside this privileged circle. Forty-two percent of rural women are illiterate and without the resources needed to "raise questions and indicate points of view" for reflection (*Lin.* preface). Struggling to survive in a world that is marked with poverty, exploitation, and lack of personhood, marriage for them is a burden and being born female a curse. Sold or off-loaded into marriage before the age of sixteen, for many of these women "the desire to marry and form a family" is not a choice (*Lin.* 1). It is a prison sentence, replete with marital rape, domestic violence, isolation, subservience to the point of slavery, and unplanned pregnancies that have fatal consequences for both mother and child.

Such women pose many challenges to the Christian vision of family. How can these women experience "the joys of human existence" when they exist in inhuman conditions (*Lin.* q. 18)? Is it possible for a woman to develop a "familial spirituality" when her every prayer is a cry of despair (*Lin.* 15)? When she has never known dignity herself, and motherhood reduces her to being a childbearer for a family of men or can be a death knell, sucking her body and her life, can she be expected to "promote the beauty and dignity of becoming a mother"? Can the indissolubility of such marriages be seen as a "gift" (*Lin.* 13)?

The answers to these questions lie not only in addressing these women's sociocultural reality but also in recognizing that their marriages are spaces of patriarchal control of their autonomy, sexuality and labor, for it is not only "market logic that prevent(s) authentic family life and leads(s) to discrimination, poverty, exclusion and violence," but also gender bias, and unless we make special efforts to promote equal partnership in the family, marriage will never be "a community of life and love" (*GS* 48).

As a woman hailing from a subcontinent where Catholics form only 1.6 percent of the population, my gaze falls also on another overlooked group of women whose numbers are increasing—women in interfaith families. Not the ones who are a triumph for the Church with their baptized children, and sometimes partners, but the ones who stand on the margins of their faith communities with their nonbaptized families and invalid marriages, the ones who are made to feel unwelcome by bishops, priests, and people.

In an attempt to give them a voice, in preparation for the 2014 Extraordinary Synod on the Family I assembled eight women to share their stories and reflect on their experiences as members, partners, and nurturers of interfaith families.[1] What I heard was an affirmation of my own story as a partner in an interfaith marriage for the past twenty-seven years, and of my belief that our marriages are not just personal choices, but also responses to the call of the Spirit to participate in a purpose and plan that goes beyond our families. As one woman said, "We are chosen; through our example people come to accept Christ."

Evangelization, however, is a two-way street. No longer confined to the religious ghetto of their birth, these Catholic "missionaries of circumstance" are challenged to embody the gospel imperative of loving discipleship. Through their participation in religious festivals and family celebrations, and reaching out in times of sickness and crises, they learn to move beyond religious labels to embrace the human person. As they witness their partners' devotion to the Divine and recognize Christ in the universal values they espouse, their worldview inevitably shifts. The unity of the baptized expands to include the unity of all God's children, and their rootedness in Christ deepens to connect with "the Word with God" (cf. John 1:1). This brings about changes in the language of their worship, the form of their rituals and their ways of doing things, in a daily living out of the "missionary option" that is more concerned about evangelizing today's world than "self-preservation" (*EG* 27).

In the process these women have learned to appreciate uniting possibilities in their interreligious relationships and to have "a more positive approach to the richness of various religious experiences" (*Lin.* 34); they have succeeded in keeping Christ alive in new ways with a faith that has remained strong despite being in the midst of an alternative religious reality, frequently without the support of their faith community; and they have come to realize that their "task is in the sowing (Mt 13:3), the rest is God's work" (*Lin.* 30).

Their rewards are the moments of grace that can so easily be overlooked—a nonbaptized, young adult accompanying his mother to the Sunday Eucharist out of choice; a Hindu husband gently nursing his bedridden, dying Catholic mother-in-law who first refused him entry into her home, then years later provided him with one. These are triumphs of the Spirit that cannot be measured by baptism.

Unfortunately, for the Church, baptism remains the defining criterion for Christian commitment. The inability to baptize children is seen as a choice *against* the Christian faith and the Church, when in reality it is a choice *for* a "vocation of love" (*Lin.* 19). The women were well aware that excluding their partner from the religious upbringing of his children and giving them a different religious "label" would alienate him and hamper the "mutual gift of self" and "creative reciprocity" that are the basis of Christian conjugal love (*Lin.* 8, 16) A form of "individualism" that seeks the benefit of one without concern for the other (*Lin.* 4), such exclusion leads to overt or covert opposition. "The Catholic Church is an invisible prison," says my Hindu husband. "Its bars cannot be seen because they are psychological." The consequences can be disastrous. "The insistence on baptism comes like a sword dividing the family," said one woman, a child of an interfaith marriage where the promise to baptize the children was made and kept, but at the cost of losing total contact with his family of birth.

In addition to questioning baptism by water as the key to Christian living as opposed to baptism of desire (*LG* 16), women in interfaith families raise many theological questions. Why is their marriage not a sacrament? Did not Christ reconcile all things in himself and redeem all marriages and families (*Lin.* 15)? Can their daily encounter of the unfathomable mystery and immensity of God as revealed in another religion be brushed aside under the pejoratives *relativism* and *syncretism*? How are their efforts to be "bold and creative" (*EG* 33) and go forth, bearing fruit and transforming situations where God has placed them, different from those of missionaries anywhere?

The *Instrumentum Laboris* of the Extraordinary Synod on the Family acknowledges that interfaith couples "bring great richness to the Church" and offer an opportunity for "growth in the Christian faith" (*IL* 78). The *Lineamenta* for the Ordinary Synod on the Family further recognizes the "possibility of fostering the spirit of...interreligious dialogue in a living together of diverse communities in the same place" (*Lin.* 6). These insights must be developed and translated into concrete action that stems from recognizing interfaith families as a sign of the times and potential avenues for evangelization.

Reexamine and revise doctrine and theology so that the doors of the Church and the sacraments are open to anyone who "moved by the Spirit, comes there looking for God" (*EG* 48); reframe laws, regulations, and liturgical practices so that they are more respectful of the "gift of love" shared by interfaith couples (*Lin.* 21); foster "welcoming communities" and pastors who will offer them support in their complex situations; provide personalized pastoral programs that encourage them in their choices and responsibilities (*Lin.* 60). Most of all, listen to what these women have to teach the Church about "the dynamics of mercy and truth that meet in Christ" (*Lin.* 10), for theirs is a "culture of encounter" that recognizes "the Lord's gratuitous work,...outside customary models" (*Lin.* questions, part 1).

NOTE

1. Astrid Lobo Gajiwala, Errol D'Lima, et al., "Report of Meeting of Women in Interfaith Families," *Vidyajyoti Journal of Theological Reflection*, 78, no. 12 (December 2014): 898–917.

READING THE SIGNS OF THE TIMES

Maternal Mortality and Reproductive Rights

NONTANDO HADEBE

In 2014, I was facilitating a discussion at a local parish in Johannesburg, South Africa on the Vatican survey on marriage and family life (*IL*).[1] The definition of "family" took up most of the time because of the diversity of family experiences among the participants. Types of families named included single-parent; child-headed; grandparent-headed; extended; divorced; same-sex unions; institutional (orphanages), and "nonfamily," as in the case of street children. The nuclear family was not the dominant model. Some participants experienced a crisis of faith brought about by the gap between their experiences of family life and the teachings of the Church, which equate family life with the nuclear family. The "discovery" of multiple forms of family came because people were given the opportunity to speak about the realities of their lives and experiences. Thus, a theology of family in this context needs to include all the multiple forms of family in order to be relevant and pastoral.

The inclusion of human experience as a source for theological reflection differentiates contextual from classical theologies.[2] Contextual theology is dynamic because it connects tradition and Scripture to ever-changing historical and cultural contexts. Classical theology is ahistorical and operates outside of context. While the inclusion of context does not necessarily challenge the teachings of the Church, it will certainly critique the application of those teachings in order to produce more liberating interpretations. That is particularly the case, not only in any discussion of the family or social problems such as poverty, HIV/AIDS, and so on, but also in the context of women's lives as mothers and bearers of life. This unique function of women defines their reproductive lives, yet for many fulfilling this function has led to their death. These deaths are the focus of the rest of the paper.

According to the World Health Organization, approximately eight hundred women die every day from preventable causes related to pregnancy and childbirth.[3] Ninety-nine percent of these deaths occur in developing countries, yet maternal mortality is hardly mentioned in Catholic social teaching documents.

The Millennium Developments Goals (MDGs) adopted in 2000 committed the international community to reduce maternal mortality by three quarters by 2015. While this target was not achieved, maternal deaths have fallen by 45 percent since 1990. However, while Catholic agencies are often in the frontline of providing health care to women and girls, the Vatican, acting through the Holy See's permanent observer status at the United Nations, has played an ambivalent and sometimes obstructive role in this project to reduce the deaths of women and girls.

The language of reproductive health and rights entered international discourse at the UN International Conference on Population and Development (ICPD) in Cairo in 1994. The Holy See agreed to this with some reservations, but it has repeatedly lobbied against extending this to include sexual rights.[4]

Reproductive rights were defined as the right to decide freely regarding family size. They were seen as a way of protecting poor communities—women in particular—from coercive population control policies. A program of action was adopted for global delivery of services that would support reproductive choice.[5] These services included family planning; antenatal care and safe delivery; prevention of abortion and management of its consequences; prevention and appropriate treatment of infertility;

information and counseling on reproductive health and care, and treatment of sexually transmitted diseases, including HIV. By framing women's reproductive health in the language of rights, the ICPD sought to recognize some of the contextual factors that contributed to the crisis that has led to the deaths of women and girls, particularly gender inequality and poverty. The defense of women's rights was thus seen as inseparable from securing women's reproductive health. The vision of ICPD continues to evolve, partly in response to opposing and supporting views from faith communities around these issues.

Responding to these new interpretations of rights, the Church has defended its understanding of marriage and family life as set out in *Humanae Vitae* (*HV*). While endorsing the rights of women and girls to education, health care, and economic justice, it has condemned the promotion of birth control and the United Nation's carefully worded advocacy of the right of access to safe abortion as being "detrimental to unborn human life and the integral needs of women and men within society."[6]

The challenge to the Church goes beyond the content of her teachings. It addresses the fundamental question of context and the voices and experiences of those who are affected by maternal death—namely, the world's poorest women and their families and communities. This is the human experience that needs to mediate the teachings of the Church, not just the agenda of ICPD. The question that remains unanswered is not how well the Church defends her position in the United Nations but how well the Church translates the experiences of women and girls into a liberating contextual theology that militates against those named factors in their lives that contribute to their deaths. By contesting UN policies relating to sexual and reproductive health and rights without any consultation with those most affected by maternal mortality, the Church missed an opportunity to engage constructively at a conceptual level with the United Nations and at a contextual level in solidarity with vulnerable women.

The exclusion or inclusion of a contextual perspective in the Church's teachings can determine whether these teachings are experienced as liberating or alienating by those most affected by them. When contextual factors are not integrated, the result is a moralistic and judgmental theology that targets actions and condemns the individuals responsible, with no pastoral sensitivity to those individuals' needs and struggles, and no respect for the role that conscience might play in their decisions. This theological approach creates a crisis of belief for the people of God and a crisis of identity for the Church, and betrays her mission to the world, which, in the words of *Gaudium et Spes*, is to respond to "the joys and the hopes, the griefs and the anxieties of the people of this age, especially those who are poor or in any way afflicted" (*GS* 1).

NOTES

1. This survey was sent to bishops around the world in preparation for the October 2014 meeting in Rome of the synod of Bishops.

2. See Stephen B. Bevans, *Models of Contextual Theology* (Maryknoll, NY: Orbis Books, 1992).

3. World Health Organization, "Maternal Mortality," fact sheet no. 348, updated May 2014, http://www.who.int/mediacen tre/factsheets/fs348/en.

4. See Tina Beattie, "Whose Rights, Which Rights?—The United Nations, the Vatican, Gender and Sexual and Reproductive Rights," *The Heythrop Journal*, 55, no. 6 (2014): 1080–90.

5. See "International Conference on Population and Development Programme of Action," UNFPA 2014, http://www.unfpa.org/publications/international-conference-population-and-development-programme-action.

6. Address of H. E. Msgr. Celestino Migliore, "Statement of the Holy See at the 64th Session of the UN General Assembly on Agenda 48: Commemoration of the International Conference of Population and Development (Cairo 1994)," October 13, 2009, http://www.vatican.va/roman_curia/secretariat_state/2009/docu ments/rc_seg-st_20091013_un-conference-cairo_en.html.

MATERNAL MIGRATION AND PATERNAL RESPONSIBILITY IN THE PHILIPPINES

Challenges for the Church

AGNES M. BRAZAL

Among the many effects of globalization on domestic life, migration has a particular impact on poor families, as women and men leave their families to seek better paid employment abroad. While in the past, transnational families consisted primarily of a male earner living apart from female and young dependents in the home country, today these families increasingly include women overseas workers with husband or children left behind.[1] The rise in the number of Asian women, and Filipino women in particular, who cross national borders to find gainful employment can be linked both to international capital's search for cheap labor and domestic services, as well as to the increasing poverty in the sending countries.[2]

However, most Filipino children, when asked to choose, say they would prefer their fathers rather than their mothers to migrate (3.6 percent vs 59.5 percent for fathers).[3] Children with migrant mothers tend to score slightly higher in anxiety and loneliness scales,[4] and they lag behind in school performance when compared to children with migrant fathers.[5] Whereas mothers who stay behind continue to care for the children, fathers who do so tend to delegate childcare to extended kin who may have children of their own or grandmothers who may be too old to raise children. Another factor is the extra work assumed by the children as a result of the mother's absence, such as household work for girls and market work for boys.

Most migrant mothers try to compensate through intensive mothering, that is, becoming supermoms and micromanaging their families via cell phones and webcams.[6] Nevertheless, migrant mothers are often vilified in news reports and frowned upon by the community. The suffering of children of overseas working mothers can be linked to society's refusal to recognize the migrant woman's efforts at redefining mothering that people traditionally expect should be done in close proximity,[7] as well as the father's refusal to take over child-rearing work and share in the household management.

When their wives leave the family to work abroad, most men face an identity crisis and diminished self-worth, as they become managers of the remittances from their wives and care-givers for their young children, tasks that have traditionally been identified as feminine. Even for men who are also earning, their income, nonetheless is usually just one-third of the remittances their wives send. A source of tension for these newfound roles of men are in-laws who look down on the men for not being able to provide for the families, thus pushing their daughters to work abroad—a suffering increased by neighbors who taunt the men for doing house and care work.

In this context of changing parental roles and economic struggles, we might reflect on church teaching about family and the gendered division of labor.

PHASE 1: LEO XIII THROUGH PIUS XII

In this first phase, the ideal Christian family is the nuclear family with a father who is employed and a mother who takes care of the home and children. In reality, however, poor working class women always had to work outside the home to augment the income of the family. The norm in this phase, nevertheless, is for the man to be the worker (*RN* 43). The women's contribution in earning a living is recognized but seen as an "abuse" that needs to be eliminated (*QA* 71).

PHASE 2: JOHN XXIII THROUGH PAUL VI

In this second phase, the model family remains the nuclear family with the man as primary breadwinner and the woman as principal caretaker. There is increasing recognition, however, that women are now working outside the home (*PT* 41), with the caution that this should not "be in contradiction with woman's proper role...at the heart of the family" (*OA* 13).

PHASE 3: JOHN PAUL II

John Paul II reinforces this gendered division of labor when he claims that "to take up paid work outside the home is wrong from the point of view of the good of society and of the family when it contradicts or hinders these primary goals of the missions of a mother" (*LE* 19.3). This directive can have the effect of adding to the burden of guilt of women who are forced to migrate. The care of the children should not be neglected, but can this be done only by the mother, and in close proximity? This teaching also reinforces the negative attitude of families and communities toward men who cannot live up to the ideal of men as the primary providers.

John Paul II's *Familiaris Consortio* (1981) directly addresses the role of men as fathers and husbands (*FC* 25), but this responsibility does not include child rearing and household management, which are tasks delegated to women (*FC* 23). It can be commended for rejecting machismo, which "humiliates women and inhibits the development of healthy family relationships" (*FC* 25) but it does not challenge that machismo that is associated with the rejection of child rearing and housework.

PHASE 4: BENEDICT XVI AND FRANCIS

With these popes, there has been no change in the doctrinal teaching, but they seem to exhibit greater fluidity regarding their views of women and men, which opens up a space for further dialogue on the role of men as fathers or husbands.

While John Paul II posits a more dualistic perspective with regard to the feminine and the masculine (*MD* 10), Cardinal Ratzinger, as then head of the Congregation for the Doctrine of the Faith, implicitly suggests a more fluid gender construction in the document, "On the Collaboration of Men and Women in the Church and in the World" (2004).[8] Here he notes that femininity as the capacity for the other is "more than simply an attribute of the female sex." While femininity for women involves—though not exclusively—the "woman's physical capacity to give life," he adds,

> The feminine values mentioned here are above all human values: the human condition of man and woman created in the image of God is one and indivisible. It is only because women are more immediately attuned to these values that they are the reminder and the privileged sign of such values. But, in the final analysis, every human being, man or woman, is destined to be for the other." (14)

For his part, Pope Francis invites Christians to have a conversation on the role of women in the church and society.[9] Implicitly, this also involves reimagining the role of men as husbands and fathers.

In the past, in the context of changing patterns of family life, the Catholic Church has revised its teachings to adapt to new situations. If as the then Cardinal Ratzinger said, femininity as the "capacity for the other" is not exclusive to women, then shouldn't the Church through its teachings encourage men to develop this capacity as well through their formation in child rearing and household management?

NOTES

1. Patricia Cortes, "The Feminization of International Migration and Its Effects on the Children Left Behind: Evidence from the Philippines," November 2011, http://fmwww.bc.edu/EC-J/SemF2011/Paper2.pdf.

2. Maruja M. B. Asis "When Men and Women Migrate: Comparing Gendered Migration in Asia," 6, paper presented to the United Nations Division for the Advancement of Women (DAW) Consultative Meeting on "Migration and Mobility and How This Movement Affects Women," Malmö, Sweden, December 2–4, 2003, http://www.un.org/womenwatch/daw/meetings/consult/CM-Dec03-EP1.pdf.

3. Victoria Paz Cruz, *Seasonal Orphans and Solo Parents: The Impacts of Overseas Migration* (Quezon City: Scalabrini Migration Center, 1987), 38.

4. Maruja M. B. Asis, *Hearts Apart: Migration in the Eyes of Filipino Children*, (Manila: ECMI-CBCP, Scalabrini Migration Center and Overseas Workers Welfare Administration, 2004), 10.

5. Cortes, "Feminization of International Migration."

6. Rachel Salazar-Parrenas, "The Gender Paradox in the Transnational Families of Filipino Migrant Women," *Asian and Pacific Migration Journal* 14, no. 3 (2005): 256–57.

7. Salazar-Parrenas, "Transnational Mothering: A Source of Gender Conflicts in the Family," https://www.academia.edu/3618761/TRANSNATIONAL_MOTHERING_A_SOURCE_OF_GENDER_CONFLICTS_IN_THE_FAMILY_.

8. Congregation for the Doctrine of the Faith, "Letter to the Bishops of the Catholic Church on the Collaboration of Men and Women in the Church," May 31, 2004, http://www.vatican.va/roman_curia/congregations/cfaith/documents/rc_con_cfaith_doc_20040731_collaboration_en.html.

9. *Zenit*, "Pope: Make More Room for Women in the Church," January 28, 2014, http://www.zenit.org/en/articles/pope-make-more-room-for-women-in-the-church.

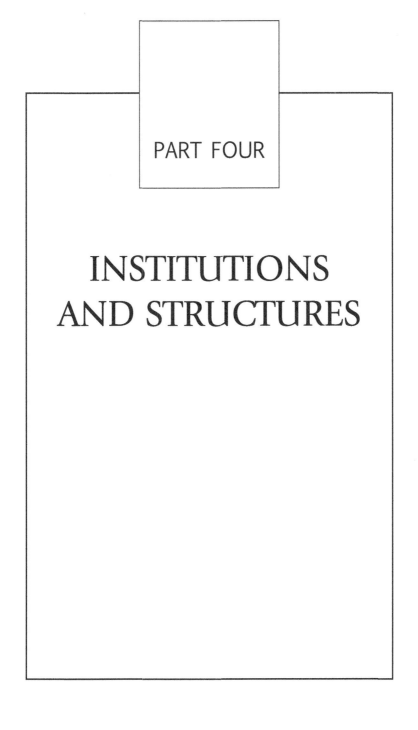

PART FOUR

INSTITUTIONS
AND STRUCTURES

INTRODUCTION
TO PART FOUR

The fourth and final section turns to church institutions, hierarchies, and structures, exposing many ways in which the absence of women limits the capacity of the institutional Church in its mission of evangelization and pastoral care. It is here that women are most invisible and silent in Catholic life.

While many Catholic communities, schools, parishes, and pastoral organizations depend upon women's participation and commitment in order to function effectively, the various forms of leadership and ministry in the Church are almost exclusively male. Not only does this exclusivity deprive the Church of women's intellectual and administrative skills, it also creates a credibility gap between the Catholic Church and most other institutions and churches in modern society, where women are increasingly able to play a full and equal part alongside men. The contributors in this section are not claiming their rights over and against men, but are committed Catholics serving the Church in many ways. They seek a deeper, richer engagement with the life of the institutional Church in equal and mutually respectful relationships with men.

Mary Aquin O'Neill draws on sociological research to question what it means to speak of women in terms of "the role of women," for "woman is not and cannot be a role." Rather, "women, like men, are capable of filling many different roles, according to our preparation and our gifts." Questioning the ways in which influential male theologians have interpreted St. Paul's understanding of the headship of Christ in relation to the Church, O'Neill appeals for a theological model that is more faithful to the Genesis understanding of the creation of woman as "helpmate" to man, a relationship in which, to cite the *Catechism*, "she thus represents God from whom comes our help" (*CCC* 1605).

Lucetta Scaraffia describes the exclusion of women from the 2014 and 2015 Synods on the Family as the Church "breathing with only one lung." She argues that the absence of women's perspectives from reflections on the family impoverishes Catholic life and contributes to the sense of "disconnect" between the practices of the faithful and Catholic moral teachings on the family. Scaraffia describes "the emancipation of women and radical change in sexual behavior" as two revolutions of the twentieth century that have far-reaching implications for the Church. In the face of the ambivalent and sometimes negative legacy of these revolutions, there is a need to redefine male and female roles. Like several other contributors to this collection, she argues that this new understanding must include a greater emphasis on men's domestic responsibilities, and affirm the Christian belief not only on the importance of the maternal role, but on equality between spouses in marriage.

Christine Schenk draws attention to the ways in which Lectionary readings are often edited to omit scriptural references to women's leadership in the Gospels and the Pauline Epistles. She asks what effect these omissions have on our sons and daughters, potentially leading young girls to internalize a sense of inferiority in relation to boys, and seeding equally damaging assumptions in boys. Schenk proposes a revision of the Lectionary texts to raise awareness "about the inclusive practice of Jesus and St. Paul through biblical preaching and proclamation."

Still on the subject of preaching, Madeleine Fredell argues that "there are many passages in the Bible that would benefit from being expounded by women." She appeals for a review of canon law so that not only ordained ministers but laywomen and -men can also preach the homily, in recognition of the fact that all the baptized are called to be "priest, prophet, and king, representing Christ to our fellow pilgrims."

Rhonda Miska explores the "blessings, challenges, and hopes" of young Catholic women's ministries, drawing on her

158

own experience of leadership in social justice and interfaith work. Such work brings blessings of "encounters and relation-ships" that "energize" young Catholics in their work. Challenges include the sometimes irresponsible exercise of priestly power and low wages, but also for women the problems of sexism that devalue women's ministries. The hope for "mil-lennials in a postmodern world" is that the Church will cre-atively engage with their struggles, in the context of Pope Francis's vision of a joyful and engaged Church which is "out on the streets" (*EG*, 49).

Finally, Catherine Cavanagh asks about the impact on family life and the perceptions of children when "Sunday after Sunday" they learn that only men can preach and read the Gospel at Mass, only men can be the *imago Christi*, that priests hold the decision-making power in the Church, that there are Fathers but no corresponding Mothers in church life, and that a host of consequences flow from these practices. Some propose the ordination of women as the answer to such problems, while others say that this is "inconceivable, even forbidden." Whatever the disagreements, Cavanagh asks that we "wrestle with the reality" in mutual trust.

ROLES FOR WOMEN
IN THE CHURCH

MARY AQUIN O'NEILL

Of late, much attention has been paid to "the role of women in the Church." Several conferences and many articles have addressed the issue, with varying results. The problem, however, lies in the use of the singular for, as Elizabeth Janeway argued persuasively many years ago, woman is not and cannot be a role.[1] Drawing on the work of sociologist Talcott Parsons, Janeway explains the components of a role and their significance for the question of "woman's role."

A role requires three dimensions: (1) a role other; (2) an activity; and (3) a social system. "Role other" refers to the person or persons for, or with whom, one performs the activity. Thus a teacher must have students, a doctor needs patients. An activity, of course, means the deed that the person in the role performs. Thus a teacher imparts information and stimulates the student to learn; the doctor heals or cares for one who is ill. Any role might have multiple activities but there must be some action that the person in the role carries out. A social system refers to the institution or network within which the person in the role functions. Most often, for instance, a teacher operates within a school, college, or university and a doctor within a hospital or clinic.

This analysis should bring important realizations. "Church" is not a single institution, but an enormous network

Initially published in Global Sisters Report, a project of *National Catholic Reporter*: www.GlobalSistersReport.org/node/26631, accessed July 25, 2015—published with permission.

of institutions that stretches from the Vatican through dioceses to parishes. Each level has its own set of systems within which one could imagine functioning. Likewise, the activities carried on cover a wide variety of possibilities. Role others will also differ according to the system within which one is operating and the activities in which one is engaged. Seen in this way, the very question, "What is woman's role in the Church?" becomes nonsensical. "Woman," as such, has no role other, no single activity, and no particular social system.

Women, like men, are capable of filling many different roles, according to our preparation and our gifts. The fact that some 80 percent of church personnel in the United States are women should be enough to show that we are already doing so. Why, then, does the question persist? Perhaps because those who think about the issue in the context of the Church are still working out of deep-seated cultural assumptions.

Janeway demonstrates that, when writers or speakers consider woman's role, they have in mind what are really three different roles: wife, mother, and housewife. (It is interesting that Pope Francis recently said that "the role of women doesn't end just with being a mother and with housework"—assuming, it seems, that all else is added on to what are universal tasks for women.)

Janeway demonstrates convincingly that, in the case of the wife, the "role other" is the husband; the "activity" involves all that constitutes conjugal relationships; and the "system" is marriage. Whereas, where the mother is concerned, the "role other" is the child or offspring; the "activity" is bearing and raising him/her/them; and the "system" is the family (today we would have to say "in whatever form that takes"). The housewife, on the other hand, finds her "role other" in an inanimate object, the house. Her activities are multiple, but all concern the keeping of the house. The system for a long time was an economic one in which the woman kept the house and the man worked outside the home to earn a living for both of them. This has changed radically, though one can't say that the one responsible for "keeping house" has changed much at all.

162

A fundamental problem with ecclesiastical reflections on the roles of women is that influential male theologians have enshrined one image used by St. Paul to characterize the relationship between Christ and his Church: "For the husband is the head of the wife just as Christ is the head of the Church, the body of which he is the Savior" (Eph 5:23). This image of the Church as "wife" to Christ has resulted in a theology of headship that rests on an assumption about the role of wife: namely, that it is a role in which the woman is always subordinate to the role other, who is the husband. Despite mammoth societal changes, few but feminist theologians have challenged the insistence on this dominant image and the way in which it has been applied to women in the Church. The conviction of subordination is, in fact, difficult to square with the *Catechism of the Catholic Church* itself. That authoritative text proclaims that the teaching of Genesis is that "the woman, 'flesh of his flesh,' i.e., his counterpart, his equal, his nearest in all things, is given to him by God as a 'helpmate'; she thus represents God from whom comes our help" (*CCC* 1605). Here, the *Catechism* reminds us that the word for "helpmate" in Genesis is a term also used for God in the Old Testament. As representative of God, then, the wife can hardly be considered under the "headship" of the husband.

Perhaps it is now clear why talk of a "theology of woman" is problematic. It is rather the case that assumptions about woman or women have had an impact on many other aspects of theology, sacramental theology and ecclesiology being the most obvious examples. Janeway's analysis drives home the need for women with a critical consciousness to be present where false assumptions about us prevail, so that those assumptions can be challenged and changed for our good and for the good of the Church.

NOTE

1. See Elizabeth Janeway, *Man's World, Woman's Place: A Study in Social Mythology* (New York: William Morrow and Co., 1971).

BREATHING WITH ONLY ONE LUNG: WHERE ARE THE WOMEN'S VOICES IN THE SYNODS?

LUCETTA SCARAFFIA

The absence of women at the 2014 and 2015 Synods on the Family reveals two negative aspects of the life of the Church: ignorance of and lack of interest in the female point of view—even in situations where women are at the heart of the matter—and disconnection from daily life.

The crisis of the family is one of the most serious and urgent of the great problems that the Church faces today. The absence of women's perspectives at times of reflection on these issues is not only an act of disdain toward women, who make up more than half of religious and believers, it is also an impoverishment of Catholic life. Unless believers really hear and put into practice the Church's teachings, the Church risks closing itself off into total self-referentiality. Without the active participation of women in discerning problems, seeking solutions, and planning for the future, the Church breathes with only one lung—it breathes badly, with difficulty.

We see this particularly with regard to the family. In the first synod, held in 2014, the problem of the "disconnect" between the practices of the faithful and Catholic moral teachings on the family—alarmingly present in all the diocesan surveys—went unaddressed. This alarm, sounded by all the bishops' conferences, should have induced the church hierarchy to enter into a serious examination of conscience on the reasons for this failure, which must include some necessary self-criticism with regard to how Church teachings are transmitted.

The synod also neglected to deal with a fundamental problem. The reasons for the crisis of the family are closely linked to two revolutions of the twentieth century: the emancipation of women and radical change in sexual behavior, phenomena that are closely related. Like all revolutions, these were brutal, forcing rapid change with radical implications, with women appearing to be the main beneficiaries. But the reality is more complex: not only did all society suffer from this transformation, but women themselves—the apparent victors—lost much. In fact, they now find themselves in a climate of ambivalence: on the one hand, they want self-realization through work; on the other hand, they do not want to give up the joys of the family, especially motherhood.

Every woman knows that, as a wife and mother, she is irreplaceable, and she obtains profound emotional gratification that is generally not comparable to what can be obtained in professional life. In today's society, it is very difficult, if not impossible, to perform both these roles—at least simultaneously. This difficulty stems not only from a lack of assistance from society and from the state, but also, and perhaps above all, from male reluctance to accept the role of husband and father—a role that is seen as a burden and a duty, lacking traditional gratifications. It is clear, therefore, that we are currently undergoing a redefinition of female and male roles, starting from the fact that for each of us to perform our shared roles well we need equal abilities and equal resources. This redefinition of roles is undoubtedly one of the newest and most complex challenges humanity must face today, and it is important that it be faced consciously, not just chaotically endured.

The Catholic tradition has much to say on this topic, starting from the doctrine of complementarity developed by Pope John Paul II and Joseph Ratzinger as prefect of the Congregation of the Doctrine of the Faith. This doctrine must, however, be submitted to a critical process of review and revision that takes into account the changes that have taken place over the past decades.

The Church could play an important constructive role in this process of change, as it is strong in two elements that have always characterized its vision of the family. The first element is equality between spouses, established for the first time in the Christian conception of marriage—equal rights and equal duties for both wife and husband. Historically, this equality was rarely or never realized, but it was undoubtedly one of the seeds of the equality that then flowered in the matrix of culturally Christian societies—the only ones from which the projects of women's emancipation and equality emerged.

The second element is the ever-vigilant attention paid to the importance and richness to humanity of the maternal role in human procreation. At the center of the problem of the new family is undoubtedly the lack of social and cultural recognition of the value of procreation, which is almost considered a burden and obstacle to individual realization, especially for women. It is as if, to be equal, women should become "men like any other," forgetting that the prospect of motherhood is something that is consubstantial with female existence.

This reality is often forgotten in a world where technology and science offer new models of human reproduction that, without yet diminishing the need for the female body (but for how long?), can fragment the maternal identity into three figures: the mother who donates the egg, the one who rents out her uterus, and the legal mother who raises the child. This reality—still experienced by a minority, but whose symbolic significance is by no means negligible—creates new forms of enslavement with regard to women's bodies.

Is this true progress for women? Is it really a new way to realize their desire for motherhood? These scientific developments confront us with many challenging questions.

If we are to begin a fruitful dialogue with women on sexuality and procreation, some questions must be clarified: feminism and science have torn procreation from nature and made it a cultural phenomenon, while the Church defends the order of nature. When it comes to sexual freedom, on the other hand, the Church for centuries has defended a strongly culturalized interpretation of sexuality, connecting feminine sexuality to Mary's virginal motherhood of Christ and to biblical and natural law concepts of monogamy, fidelity, and female submissiveness, while proponents of sexual liberalism proclaim that to be "natural."

Church synods must deal with these fundamental issues. We need women to present a feminine point of view, not just to be considered as an opposing party advancing claims, but as an essential part of the work of theological development. If the Church's voice is to be heard, women must share the work of proclamation.

IT'S NOT ALL ABOUT EVE: WOMEN IN THE LECTIONARY

CHRISTINE SCHENK

Until recent centuries most historical texts—including the Old and New Testaments—were written by men. It is therefore not surprising that Lectionary readings in both Protestant and Catholic churches are mainly about male biblical figures. When women's stories are included, the selections and attendant preaching invariably reflect what men think about women rather than what women themselves thought or did in biblical times.

WHICH WOMEN'S STORIES DO WE HEAR?

Consider, for example, a Lectionary omission in Holy Week. In Matthew's Gospel (26:6–13), just before the passage we read on Palm Sunday in Year A, there is the story of a woman who takes the prophetic leadership role of anointing Jesus' head, much as Samuel once anointed King David. Yet her story is excluded from the Palm Sunday and Wednesday of Holy Week readings, even though Jesus, after rebuking the male disciples for criticizing her generous act, is recorded as saying, "Truly I tell you,

Edited article reprinted from *America*, July 6, 2009, with permission of America Press, Inc., (2009). All rights reserved. For subscription information, call 1-800-627-9533 or visit www.americamagazine.org.

wherever this good news is proclaimed in the whole world, what she has done will be told in remembrance of her."

While Mark's version of the anointing woman's story is part of the Gospel passage for Palm Sunday in Year B, it may be omitted, making it possible for us never to hear about this woman's prophetic gesture that must have been very consoling to Jesus. It is hard to imagine a similar directive from Jesus involving a male disciple being deleted or made optional for over two thousand years. Unfortunately, the anointing passage we do hear about regularly is the one in which a forgiven female sinner washes and anoints Jesus' feet with her hair (Luke 7:36–50). We hear about her on the 11th Sunday in Ordinary Time, Year C, and every year on Thursday of the 24th week in Ordinary Time. The selectivity seen in the choice of anointing passages gives the impression that women and sin are invariably linked.

WOMEN, JESUS, AND ST. PAUL

Contemporary biblical scholarship has uncovered important roles held by women in the early Jesus movement. Catholic women and men are edified to learn that Jesus included women in his Galilean discipleship and that women received the first commission to proclaim the Resurrection. Luke 8:1–3 tells us that Mary of Magdala, Joanna, Susanna, and many other women accompanied Jesus and ministered with him in Galilee. Yet this Lukan reading is rarely heard on Sunday, since it is optional on the 11th Sunday in Ordinary Time in Year C. Mary of Magdala's commissioning to "go and tell my brothers" that Jesus has risen (cf. John 20:10–18) does not appear on Easter or on any Sunday of the Easter season in the United States but is relegated to Easter Tuesday.

Many Catholics mistakenly believe that St. Paul was anti-woman. Yet, as Pope Benedict XVI said in his February 14, 2007 address, St. Paul worked closely with women leaders like Phoebe, Junia, Lydia, and Prisca. Unfortunately, Romans 16, a passage that names ten women and identifies some of them as deacons, apostles, and coworkers, is never proclaimed on a Sunday. Nor are the accounts of women leaders in the Acts of the Apostles (Lydia, Prisca, Tabitha), which are read only on the weekdays of Easter. As a result, most Catholics never hear about these important women who minister alongside Paul and Peter.

And where are the biblical stories of the strong women leaders of salvation history? Couldn't we include the story of Shiprah and Puah, the Hebrew midwives who saved a nation of boy children, perhaps even Moses, by defying Pharaoh's law to kill all male infants born to the enslaved Hebrews? Currently the Lectionary version of Exodus 1:8–22 (Monday of the 15th Week in Ordinary Time, Year I) excises these valiant women by inexplicably omitting verses 15 to 21.

Proclaiming Lectionary texts that exclude or distort the witness of women, particularly in a church where all priestly liturgical leadership is male, is dangerous for our daughters and our sons. Young girls can hardly avoid internalizing the notion that God must have created them less important than their brothers. If all-male liturgical leadership and Sunday Lectionary readings are subtly seeding subordination in our daughters, what is being planted in our sons?

AFTER THE SYNOD ON THE WORD

At the 2008 Synod on the Word, for the first time in history, Catholic bishops "recognized and encouraged" the ministry of women of the word and discussed the need to restore women's stories to the Lectionary. Synod Proposal 16 recommended taking a new look at the Lectionary to "see if the actual selection and ordering of the readings are truly adequate to the mission of the Church in this historic moment."[1]

To date, there has been no follow-up to this important proposal. A feasible next step would be to convene a gender-balanced group of biblical scholars and liturgists to decide which women's stories would be most fruitful for prayer, preaching, and catechesis. Church leaders could restore women like Phoebe (Rom 16:1–2), Lois and Eunice (2 Tim 1:4),

Shiprah and Puah (Exod 1:8–22), and Mary of Magdala (John 20:11–18) to Lectionary texts from which they have been deleted and consider adding the stories of other prominent biblical leaders like Esther, Deborah, Huldah, and Judith.

Raising awareness about the inclusive practice of Jesus and St. Paul through biblical preaching and proclamation is a worthy and achievable goal for our Church right now. Such renewed awareness witnesses to the truth that Jesus' saving power can heal a deeply rooted sexism that distorts the God in whose image both women and men are made.

NOTE

1. Synod of Bishops, "The Word of God in the Life and Mission of the Church" (*Instrumens Laboris*), 2008, http://www.vat ican.va/roman_curia/synod/documents/rc_synod_doc_20080511_ instrlabor-xii-assembly_en.html.

"THE APOSTLE TO THE APOSTLES"

Women Preaching the Good News

MADELEINE FREDELL

Among the earliest believers in Jesus Christ were women who actively proclaimed the good news. As we still have their stories and sometimes even their names, we can draw the conclusion that they were highly esteemed and most certainly listened to.

Given the epithet *apostle to the apostles*, Mary from Magdala is the foremost role model of preaching the homily in the Church. She was the first person sent by our Lord to proclaim the good news of his resurrection. The encounter between Jesus and the Samaritan woman urges her to proclaim the good news of the arrival of the Messiah to her fellow citizens and "many Samaritans from that city believed in him because of the woman's testimony," says the Evangelist (John 4:39). St. Paul has even given us the names of three outstanding women who by their ministries preached the good news, Phoebe, a deaconess; Prisca, a coworker; and Junia, an apostle.

On several occasions, Pope Francis has said that the Church needs to listen to women's voices. He admits that the problem goes deeper than a pure "functionalism" so it is not only about assigning leadership positions to women. The Church is in need of a cultural change, a change of mentality, the kind of mental transformation that the Canaanite woman conveys to Jesus in Matthew's Gospel. When she says "even the dogs eat the crumbs that fall from their masters' table" (Matt 15:27), she causes

Jesus to question his belief that he is only sent to the lost sheep of the house of Israel. Listening to women's voices is about getting as broad a picture as possible of how God is acting in and with our reality. Therefore, we cannot settle for listening only to priests' homilies; we need women in the pulpit as well.

There are many passages in the Bible that would benefit from being expounded by women, such as the story of the woman who had suffered from a hemorrhage for twelve years (Mark 5:25–34). Might a woman preacher ask us to reflect on how it feels to know that women were excluded from the counting of those present at the miracle of the loaves and fishes, when Mark's Gospel refers to "five thousand men" (Mark 6:44) and Matthew's Gospel tells us that "and those who ate were about five thousand men, besides women and children" (Matt 14:21)?

All the baptized are encouraged to proclaim the gospel in their everyday lives as part of God's own mission in the world. The homily however is the principal locus where most faithful Christians hear the gospel message translated into their own context. In our time, we need convincing interpretations of the texts. To achieve this we need both men and women to be preachers. It is from the pulpit we ought to be reminded of the gospel as a subversive memory in and for our own time. Men's and women's experiences are equally important here.

As a member of the Order of Preachers, I am an heir to the first community of women that St. Dominic founded, called "The Holy Preaching." Preaching is our fundamental vocation as Dominicans. One of our primary role models is St. Catherine of Siena, who was listened to by laypeople, priests, bishops, and popes. She was a forerunner of a theology based on lived experiences and that is why she is relevant even today, but she and her contemporaries were never given the opportunity to preach during Mass. Still today, we are only listening to priests' interpretations of the good news and their views of the situations we face.

It is time to ask ourselves if the homily really has to be related to the ordained ministry in the Church. According to Canon Law 762–64 only deacons and priests have the right to give the homily. This calls for a review of canon law in order

173

to give the baptized the right to listen to laywomen's and -men's interpretation of the good news today. There are many biblical stories that relate directly to women's experiences in different areas of daily life, but there are also passages that would be given a new dimension by a woman's voice. Many people, and especially women, have a long history of subordination and therefore can expound the meaning of Jesus' words to his disciples regarding the exercise of power: "But it is not so among you" (Mark 10:43). If we are serious about the Christian paradigm we cannot allow ourselves to imitate the secular patterns of power and careerism.

The Church can no longer forego women's experiences and at the same time remain trustworthy in its proclamation of the good news. Women themselves want to give voice to their worldviews and not be interpreted through a male lens. We are baptized to be priest, prophet, and king, representing Christ to our fellow pilgrims. This has to be translated into practice.

The Swedish Lutheran church has an institution called *venia*, which authorizes a layperson, woman or man, to give a homily during the main religious service on Sundays. *Venia* is given by the local bishop for the diocese or by the parish priest for the parish to a competent person. This kind of institution could be a way forward also in the Catholic Church to allow women with suitable formation to give a homily at Sunday Masses and Holy Days and expound the mysteries of faith.

This is one way to avoid the pure functionalism that Pope Francis has warned us of. With laypeople in the pulpit, we will go out to the margins of the Church and we will hear the stories of the Church as a "field hospital" and be reminded of our first duty, to heal the wounds of the poor. Our role model is Mary from Magdala both for women and for men in the pulpit.

YOUNG CATHOLIC WOMEN WORKING IN MINISTRY

Blessings, Challenges, and Hopes

RHONDA MISKA

While I cannot claim to speak for all young professional women in Catholic ministry, these reflections draw on my own experience as well as insights gleaned from many conversations. Prayers for vocations are being answered through young Catholic women—lay and religious—committed to living the gospel and serving God's people as ecclesial ministers. In the words of a ministry peer, "When I was fourteen I felt a call to lay ecclesial ministry, and it didn't leave me. I heard the call and was shown it was possible." As young professional Catholic women we experience both profound blessings and significant challenges; we hold vibrant hopes for the Church as we look to the future.

BLESSINGS

As women, we are uniquely able to respond to the needs of other women. As younger people, we are generally energetic and idealistic. In many cases, we are tech savvy and good at engaging social media—valuable skills in today's Church and world.

We serve in a wide range of ministries. We are not only youth ministers or directors of religious education as is sometimes assumed because of our age, nor are we only administrative staff as is sometimes assumed because of our gender. As a minister, I have been privileged to come alongside parishioners navigating situations including crisis pregnancies, domestic violence, medical emergencies, detention and deportation of family members, as well as those experiencing less drastic but nonetheless significant experiences, including the diminishments of aging, children leaving home, and other life transitions.

Two ministry experiences stand out as I reflect on the blessings of my call. While serving as a social justice minister, I coordinated the transformation of the parish activity center into a temporary shelter for fifty homeless men. Community was spontaneously created among the guests and the parishioners in the sharing of stories, songs, meals, and clean-up duties. Night after night, I fell into bed exhausted and grateful for the ways I witnessed the kingdom become so clearly visible. Also as social justice minister, I served on the leadership of an interfaith congregation-based community organization. At an action meeting before 1,600 people, I stood beside a Spanish-speaking, low-income parishioner giving testimony and interpreted her words into English about the lack of adequate public transportation in her neighborhood.

These are holy moments for which I still feel deep awe and gratitude. To walk with people through the pastoral cycle, bearing witness to continual conversion and growth in holiness—and to be transformed ourselves in the process—is profoundly beautiful. These encounters and relationships are the blessings that energize us.

CHALLENGES

Some challenges we face are not unique to us but are shared by many ministers. Though there is a great tradition in Catholic social teaching of upholding dignity of work and rights of workers, sadly this is not always practiced in Catholic workplaces. There are too many stories of a new priest or bishop being assigned and making major changes—including firings—without consultation and, often, without opportunities for mediation. Morality clauses required of Catholic employees are problematic, causing division in workplaces and driving away talented ministers. Low wages that come with ministry positions are especially challenging for young people paying off student loans and other debt.

Other challenges are unique to women, sometimes exacerbated by the fact that we are younger. As one peer says, "It's not easy to be an authority *and* a woman *and* young in the Church." Another peer articulates a frustration many of us share: "I know my gifts and talents, but I truly feel like in many situations they are ignored because I don't wear a collar." Many of us have experienced blatant sexism in professional settings. I was directly told by a priest that pastoral ministry was something nice to do until I started my "real" life's work: marriage and motherhood.

As women raised in the 1970s and 1980s, we were taught that there was no limit to what we could be when we grew up. The Church is one of the last places where that rings false and where we struggle to be seen as what we are: professional Catholic women, serving in ministry. This tension becomes particularly clear in interfaith settings, working alongside women leaders in other traditions; do we "count" as clergy or not?

While I personally have never felt a call to ordination, I have seen peers (after much difficult discernment) seek ordination in other denominations. This is a tremendous loss to the Church because these are smart, committed, talented women. I trust their response to God's call, yet it saddens me that they have to leave their tradition in order to serve.

HOPES

As young Catholic professional women, we find inspiration in the words and action of Pope Francis: his humility, simplicity, joy, and willingness to engage in tough questions and critique ecclesial structures. One ministry peer says, "Pope Francis gives me such hope....He leads with such love and compassion." The ecclesiology presented in *Evangelii Gaudium* resonates with our own ministerial experiences as well as our intuitions of what the future is calling forth. We join Pope Francis in envisioning a Church that is joyful, engaged, outwardly focused, and "out on the streets" (*EG*, 49).

We hope for the acknowledgment of our dignity as women with a call to ministry and for the respect of our voices and experiences. The blessings that enlarge our hearts and the challenges that wound us are equally real. Many of us have been deeply formed in, and treasure the riches of, different streams of Catholic tradition—Franciscan, Ignatian, Dominican. As millennials in a postmodern world, we appreciate the deep, rich grounding our Catholic identity offers. We have been graced in our encounters with God mediated by the Church and treasure our calls. And yet our experiences of sexism and injustice within that Catholic identity create internal struggles. We hope our naming of that struggle can be heard and creatively engaged.

ON ELEPHANTS, ANGELS, AND TRUST

The Structure of the Church and Catholic Families

CATHERINE CAVANAGH

This article is an act of trust.

The topic is the "elephant in the room"—the "Great Unspoken."

I trust that you will read on anyway, for we are in this together.

What does the Church teach us through its very structure about men, women, and families? The words of our Catholic faith teach us deep lessons of love, dignity, and life. But our children also internalize other messages, not so positive, left unspoken sometimes, but unmistakably reinforced and lived out in the fabric of the Church. There are difficult questions that arise from this, questions we would like to avoid, questions that make us nervous, but questions that—like a herd of bellowing elephants—will not be ignored.

What is the impact on the family of a Church where Sunday after Sunday only men preach? How does it affect the family to be told that only men can be the *imago Christi*? And what is it like to have all the decisions at the upper echelons of the Church made by men?

Consider just the following four teachings of the Church and their consequences:

1. **Only men can be priests, *in persona Christi*.**

   Possible consequences for the family: Dad must be more important than Mom. In general, God must think boys are more important than girls. Sure, Mary is awesome, but she is not God. Christ is God and that makes God male and priests male (forget our teaching that all are created in the image of God.) So males come first, and females come second.

2. **Only men can read the Gospel at Mass and preach.**

   Possible consequences for the family: Men's voices are more important than women's. In the family, Dad's voice must be more important than Mom's. Men must have more interesting things to say; they must be brighter, more articulate, more worthy of being heard. At the most extreme, male experience alone covers all the important aspects of human experience.

3. **The positions with greatest decision-making power in the Church are all held by priests.**

   Possible consequences for the family: Men are perceived as better decision-makers than women. Dad's word is final, Mom's is tentative. And priests must be better decision-makers than laypeople. Therefore, whatever the actual teachings, laypeople should just accept without question the decisions of the ordained. Thus, issues of great importance—like sex abuse for instance—are too often left in the hands of priests or bishops with conflicting agendas. Laypeople—families—have conceded authority to protect their children to the Church at their own peril.

4. **In the parish, someone is "Father." There is no corresponding "Mother."**

   Possible consequences for the family: There is no tangible role in the Church for women complementary to that of priest. Nor are the feminine

traits of God given the weight of "God the Father."
Therefore, men are perceived as self-sufficient
(independent of women) and fathers are more
important than mothers. Men do not need
women.

Have we done enough to mitigate the possible consequences named above? The evidence suggests not. These teachings have supported a multitude of double standards. If women
dress in beautiful clothes, they are vain. If priests dress in beautiful robes, they reflect the majesty of the Church. If women
confess a call to preach, they are accused of either being hungry
for power, or being delusional. If men confess a call to preach,
they are warmly welcomed to a process of discernment. Every
parish offers ministry and sacraments through a male person,
and that priest is under the direction of another man, and so on
up. No woman is deemed capable of offering the sacraments,
let alone participating as an equal in the magisterium.

But there is worse. These practices undermine the value of
women within society, and more importantly within their own
hearts. They assert the importance of women's obedience to
husbands and fathers. Women who do not obey the men in
their lives (or even their communities) are vulnerable to
assault, rape, even murder. Even in North America, with its relative affluence and stability, one in four women is sexually
assaulted, sometimes by a member of her own family. We are
the largest religion in the world. If men are in charge of the
Church, and the Church is the supreme model of society and
the family, then the Church broadcasts the message that in fact
men *should* be in charge of women, including their bodies.
Despite the words of love we use, of equality and dignity, in our
practice our Church at times reinforces the diminished status of
women and increases their vulnerability with dire consequences.

What then, do we do with all the wonderful teachings that
say men and women are both created equal in the image of
God? What do we do with teachings about the steadfast love of

God for all? Where is this God in the practice of the Church? In short, how do we put the *words* of our faith—those that affirm the dignity of all—into the *practice* of our faith?

Some propose answers that seem inconceivable, even forbidden. Ordain women. Let them preach. Welcome them (and married men too) to the magisterium. Make the gathering of the Mass one of equals. Recognize the *imago Christi* beyond male or female.

We may disagree on those answers. But let us agree at least, all of us, to wrestle with the questions. Let us not ask what is impossible, but rather what is possible. Let us wrestle with the reality. Let us wrestle like Jacob with this God of all that is always here, that lives in angels, messengers, and prophets— men and women. Let each of us trust the other to wrestle.

For I do believe our God is here, now, in this Church, in this world. The Spirit of our God lives in our hearts, and calls us to answer the difficult questions. We can neither look away nor pretend we do not hear their beckoning. At the very least, let us acknowledge the elephants in our midst. And then let us look for the angels too.

Christ was born of a woman who answered a divine call, and yet lived in a world where women were frequently outcast, marginalized, and rejected—the same world many women live in now. He sought them out, brought them back fully into community, listened to them, empowered them, and finally, after the resurrection, sent a woman—Mary Magdalene—out first to proclaim the good news.

As Church, it is time we do the same. Not just for women, men, children, and families, but ultimately to walk more closely in the footsteps of God.

EPILOGUE

EDITORIAL TEAM

The foregoing is a chorus of women's voices from many cultures, contexts, ages, and stages in life. Some are published theologians, others are telling their personal stories for the first time. Though we vary widely in our perspectives and experiences, we have in common our Catholic faith and a desire to participate in the Church's vocation to incarnate Christ within the cultures and communities of this global era. We bring many different gifts to the table, as we seek to celebrate the fecundity of our faith, to share our struggles and frustrations, and to witness to the "unruly freedom of the word, which accomplishes what it wills in ways that surpass our calculations and ways of thinking" (*EG* 22).

From the beginning, this work has been sustained in prayer by many more women than those who have contributed to the book. It has been a project of passionate commitment and collaboration, sparked by a desire to bring women's voices to the table for the Synod on the Family in October 2015, and taking only seven weeks from conception to completion. It is a shared endeavor, graced by a sense of "rightness" about its timing and relevance. In solidarity with one another and working together, we have tried to share our knowledge and to tell our stories with trust and honesty, bringing theological reflection to bear on intimate experiences of love and loss, failure and hope, painful endings and new beginnings. We have expressed ourselves in ways that make us vulnerable to criticism from inside and outside the Church. Some in the Church might see us as too challenging in the questions we raise and the dilemmas we acknowledge. Many who have left the Church might wonder why we stay, when we admit to so many difficulties.

We stay because we love the Church, and we belong within the sacramental body of Christ. We trust in the infinite compassion and love of the Christ who reached out to his women disciples in healing, welcome, and friendship. We draw inspiration from the many women named in the Bible, from the women saints, martyrs, and mystics who have kept the candle of women's wisdom aglow, and from the anonymous women of every age and culture who have enriched our world through quiet daily acts of love and faithfulness.

We keep watch with Mary in the time of annunciation, awaiting the new life that comes with the conception of a child or the dawning of a vision (Luke 1:26–38). Young and old together, we rejoice with Mary and Elizabeth at the wonders God has worked for us in calling us and blessing us as we walk the rocky road of love's enduring faithfulness (Luke 1:39–56). We learn patience and discernment as we reflect upon the widowed prophet Anna, finally encountering the one she was waiting for in her eighty-fourth year (Luke 2:36–38). We draw inspiration from Mary's initiative and insight at the wedding at Cana when, recognizing that the time was right and braving her Son's rebuke, she told the servants to "do whatever he tells you" (John 2:1–10). We anoint Jesus's feet with our perfume and our tears, and he welcomes us even when our religious leaders are scandalized by our behavior (Luke 7:37–39). We walk to the well in the heat of the day with the Samaritan woman, for the one that we encounter there knows all our stories of lost loves and broken relationships, and he is not ashamed to be seen with us (John 4:7–28). Like the Syrophoenician woman we pester Jesus on behalf of our daughters, and he admires us for our wit and rewards us for our persistence (Mark 7:24–30). We too experience the hunger for knowledge that made Mary want to talk theology with Jesus rather than help her sister in the kitchen, but we also experience the irritation of Martha at being left alone to do the cooking (Luke 10:38–42). We share with those two sisters the bitter disappointment when Jesus does not

184

come to take away the horror of illness and death, and we wonder how they felt when Jesus wept and called forth Lazarus from the tomb (John 11:1–44). We reach out to touch the hem of Christ's garment when our bodies are bleeding and we feel the pain of rejection and blame (Luke 8:43–48). We sit at the Passover table as Christ anticipates the suffering and joy to come in the language of childbirth, and we know that he shares the vulnerability and strength of our womanly bodies (John 16:21–22). We draw courage from the immensity of sorrow and faithfulness of Mary and her woman companions at the foot of the cross (John 19:25). We keep vigil with the women through the long and empty hours of Holy Saturday. We arise early in the morning with them to go out and anoint the bodies of our beloved dead, and we open ourselves to the unexpected encounter with newness and life outside the empty tomb (Luke 24:1–8). We hear our names spoken in the garden of the resurrection, and Jesus sends us out with wings on our heels to tell the world that our beloved is risen (John 20:11–18). He is here. He is with us. He has birthed us into a new creation and given us a song to sing and a message to tell that resounds from our fledgling beginnings in the garden of Eden to our glorious fulfilment in the City of God.

We join with the women of the early Church—Lydia, Prisca, Phoebe, Junia, Thecla, Perpetua, Felicity, Egeria, Eudokia, Macrina; with medieval abbesses, saints, mystics, and martyrs—Lioba, Walburg, Hilda of Whitby, Brigid of Ireland, Hrotsvit, Bridget of Sweden, Clare of Assisi, Mechthild of Magdeburg, Julian of Norwich, Hadewijch of Antwerp, Joan of Arc, Elizabeth of Hungary, Gertrud of Helfta, Heloise, Marguerite Porete; with women missionaries and founders of religious institutes and movements dedicated to social justice, evangelization, and human development—Angela Merici, Mary Ward, Jeanne de Lestonnac, Catherine McAuley, Mary Elizabeth Lange, Jeanne Jugan, Nano Nagle, Anna Dengel, Mary Ann Seton, Mary MacKillop, Marianne Cope, Kateri Tekakwitha, Janet Stuart, Mary Potter, Josephine Bakhita, Dorothy Day, Chiara Lubich, and with women doctors of the Church—Teresa of Ávila, Catherine of Siena, Thérèse of Lisieux, Hildegard of Bingen. We join our visions and our prayers with theirs across vast distances of time and space, knowing that we belong within a hidden seam of gold in the Church's theological tradition as we continue to speak of God in the language of women's visions and experiences of faith.

Come, those of you who would like to accompany us. Take our hands and join with us as we journey together in trust and communion, as pilgrims who "turn our gaze to what we are all seeking: the radiant peace of God's face" (*EG* 244). Let's "come together to take charge of this home which has been entrusted to us, knowing that all the good which exists here will be taken up into the heavenly feast," and "Let us sing as we go. May our struggles and our concern for this planet never take away the joy of our hope" (*LS* 244).